Library Research Guide to Psychology

"Library Research Guides" Series

JAMES R. KENNEDY, JR. and
THOMAS G. KIRK, JR., Editors

No. 1   LIBRARY RESEARCH GUIDE TO
                RELIGION AND THEOLOGY

No. 2   LIBRARY RESEARCH GUIDE TO BIOLOGY

No. 3   LIBRARY RESEARCH GUIDE TO EDUCATION

No. 4   LIBRARY RESEARCH GUIDE TO HISTORY

No. 5   LIBRARY RESEARCH GUIDE TO SOCIOLOGY

No. 6   LIBRARY RESEARCH GUIDE TO MUSIC

No. 7   LIBRARY RESEARCH GUIDE TO PSYCHOLOGY

Library Research Guide to Psychology

Illustrated Search Strategy and Sources

by
NANCY E. DOUGLAS
Reference Librarian
Texas A&M University

and
NATHAN BAUM
Head, Cataloging with Copy Dept.
State Univ. of N.Y., Stony Brook

("Library Research Guides" Series, No. 7)

Pierian Press
ANN ARBOR, MICHIGAN

Copyright © 1984 by The Pierian Press. All rights reserved.

International Standard Book Numbers: 0-87650-156-0 (cloth)
                                       0-87650-175-7 (paper)
Library of Congress Catalog Card Number: LC 84-60640

Pierian Press, P.O. Box 1808, Ann Arbor, Michigan 48106
Printed in the United States of America

Contents

Preface	vii
Acknowledgements	vii
Introduction	xi

1.
Choosing Your Topic — 1

2.
Communicating with the Card Catalog — 7

3.
Reviews of the Literature: *Annual Review of Psychology* — 13

4.
The Subject Approach and Computer Searching: *Social Sciences Index, Psychological Abstracts,* and "Permuterm Index" of *Social Sciences Citation Index* — 17

5.
The Author Approach: *Social Sciences Citation Index* — 29

6.
The Last Six Months: *Current Contents* — 33

7.
Using Guides to the Literature of Psychology — 37

8.
Using other Libraries — 41

Appendix I
Library Knowledge Test — 43

Appendix II
Index Medicus — 45

Appendix III
Monthly Catalog — 48

Appendix IV
Basic Reference Sources for Psychology Courses — 51
   Outline
   Bibliography

Appendix V
Guidelines for Proceeding — 63

Index — 65

Preface

Is This the Book You Need?

The answer is yes if you find yourself in one of the following situations:

1. You are a college student majoring in psychology who needs to know how to locate appropriate library materials for term papers. This book assumes the card catalog and the *Readers' Guide to Periodical Literature* (New York: Wilson, 1905–) are "old friends," but you need to be introduced to the basic reference sources for psychology. If, by some chance, you do not know how to use the card catalog and the *Readers' Guide* well, or have not written term papers for other courses that provided good library experiences, then read the warning in the last two paragraphs of this preface.

2. You are a graduate student in psychology who will be writing a number of research papers. This book will guide you to many useful reference sources.

3. You are a professor of psychology or a reference librarian to whom students often come for advice on how to find library materials for term papers in psychology. This book will be helpful in supplying that advice.

Caveat Lector (Let the Reader Beware)

Do not begin this book if:

1. You have not learned how to use the card catalog and the *Readers' Guide*. Take the five-minute, self-graded test in Appendix I to test your knowledge. If you do poorly on the test, save this book until you have read the pages explaining the card catalog and the *Readers' Guide* in such books as Margaret G. Cook, *The New Library Key*, 3d ed. (New York: Wilson, 1975); or Ella Aldrich, *Using Books and Libraries*, 5th ed. (Englewood Cliffs, NJ: Prentice-Hall, 1967).

2. You need to know the general procedures for writing term papers, including note-taking, outlining, and bibliographical forms. Use this book in conjunction with Kate L. Turabian, *Students' Guide for Writing College Papers*, 3d ed., rev. (Chicago: University of Chicago Press, 1976); or Lucille Hook and Mary V. Gaver, *The Research Paper*, 4th ed. (Englewood Cliffs, NJ: Prentice-Hall, 1969); or Robert J. Sternberg, *Writing the Psychology Paper* (Woodbury, NY: Baron's Educational Series, 1977).

Acknowledgments

Many people, more than we can name here, generously provided us with assistance and encouragement while this book was being prepared. We are indebted to them all. We would especially like to thank Kathy Jackson, Leila Payne, and many other library staff members at Texas A&M University and the State University of New York at Stony Brook for their continued encouragement and patience; Dr. William S. Rholes of the Psychology Department at Texas A&M and Dr. Xenia Coulter of the Psychology Department at SUNY Stony Brook for taking the time to read the manuscript and share ideas with us; and Scott McCullar for his tailor-made cartoons.

We are especially grateful and indebted to Tom Kirk and Jim Kennedy for the guidance in format and substance provided by their own books in the Library Research Guide Series, particularly for the early chapters of our book. To them, too, we are thankful for the time and concerned effort expended in editing this book. Of course, we remain responsible for any errors or omissions.

Credits for Figures

Thanks are due to the many publishers cited below who gave their permission to use excerpts from copyrighted works. Without their courtesy this book could not have been the illustrated guide that was intended. Uncopyrighted materials are also cited below in order to make the list of figures complete.

FIGURES 1.1–1.3: From *International Encyclopedia of Psychiatry, Psychology, Psychoanalysis, & Neurology*. 12 vols. Copyright 1977. Used with permission of Aesculapius Publishers, Inc. FIGURE 1.2 also used with permission of Percy H. Tannenbaum.

FIGURE 1.3: From *International Encyclopedia of the Social Sciences*. 18 vols. Copyright 1968. Crowell Collier and Macmillan, Inc. Used with permission of Macmillan Publishing Co., Inc.

FIGURE 2.1: United States Library of Congress catalog card.

FIGURE 2.2: United States Library of Congress. *Library of Congress Subject Headings*. 9th ed., 1980.

FIGURE 2.3: United States Library of Congress catalog cards.

FIGURES 3.1–3.3: From the *Annual Review of Psychology*. vols. 28 and 30. Copyright 1977 and 1979. Used with permission of Annual Reviews, Inc. FIGURE 3.3 also used with permission of Robert Liebert.

FIGURE 4.1: From *Social Science Index*. June 1980 issue. Copyright 1980. Used with permission of The H.W. Wilson Company.

FIGURES 4.2–4.3: From *Psychological Abstracts*. vols. 66 and 63. Copyright 1981 and 1980. Used with the permission of the American Psychological Association.

FIGURES 4.4–4.5: From the *Thesaurus of Psychological Index Terms*, 3d ed. Copyright 1982. Used with the permission of the American Psychological Association.

FIGURES 4.6–4.8: From *Psychological Abstracts*. vol. 65. Copyright 1981. Used with permission of the American Psychological Association.

FIGURE 4.9: From *Sociological Abstracts*. vol. 26. Copyright 1978. Used with permission of Sociological Abstracts, Inc.

FIGURES 4.10–4.12: From *Social Sciences Citation Index Five Year Cumulation 1971–1975*. Copyright 1979. Used with permission of the Institute for Scientific Information.

FIGURES 4.13–4.14: From Bibliographical Retrieval Services PSYC database. Used with permission of Bibliographical Retrieval Services, Inc.

FIGURE 5.1: How a citation is indexed in *Social Sciences Citation Index*. A portion from the *International Social Science Journal*, vol. 30, no. 4. Copyright 1978. Used with permission of UNESCO.

FIGURES 5.2–5.5: From *Social Sciences Citation Index 1979 Annual*. Copyright 1979. Used with permission of the Institute for Scientific Information.

FIGURES 6.1–6.3: From *Current Contents/Social & Behavioral Sciences*. vol. 12, no. 28, 14 July 1980. Copyright 1980. Used with permission of the Institute for Scientific Information.

FIGURE 6.4: From *Current Contents/Social & Behavioral Sciences*. vol. 14, no. 1, 1982. Used with permission of the Institute for Scientific Information.

FIGURE 7.1: From *A Guide to Library Research in Psychology*, by James E. Bell. Copyright 1971. Used with permission of James E. Bell.

FIGURE 7.2: From *Sources of Information in the Social Sciences*, by Carl M. White. Copyright 1973, American Library Association. Used with permission of the American Library Association and Carl M. White.

FIGURE 7.3: From *Guide to Reference Books, Supplement*, by Eugene P. Sheehy. Supplement to 9th ed. 1980.

FIGURE 8.1: From *Library of Congress Subject Catalog*,

1978.

FIGURE II.1: From *Index Medicus*, June 1980.

FIGURES II.2–II.4: From *Medical Subject Headings*, 1980.

FIGURE II.5: From *Index Medicus*, June 1980.

FIGURES III.1–III.3: From *Monthly Catalog of U.S. Government Publications*, 1980.

Introduction

The Frustrations of a Term Paper

"A term paper will be due the last week of the course." If you are like most students who hear these words on the first day of class, you wish you had known enough to have chosen another course. It is not that you are a loafer. You just know from previous experience that, to get a decent grade on a term paper, you will have to cope once again with that monument to frustration, your college or university library. Never yet have you managed to find those two essentials: a topic that really captures your interest and the right books and articles to stimulate and satisfy your curiosity about the topic. Sometimes you have come close, but not without spending tedious hours thumbing through the card catalog and browsing in the stacks.

Our Purpose and Method

Writing a term paper may never be easy, but it can be made much easier if you learn to use an effective *search strategy* and the appropriate reference sources. That is what this book is all about.

A search strategy is simply an organized way of finding an appropriate term paper topic and then finding enough important library materials on that topic. As this book will show, search strategy involves much, much more than just looking up a few titles in the card catalog.

This book is designed to teach basic search strategy and reference sources by leading you through a search, using a typical psychology term paper topic as an example. Excerpts from the most useful reference sources relate to the sample topic and demonstrate both search strategy and the use of these sources. This teaching method gives you a model which you can readily adapt to your own topic.

The Goal of This Book

Students are usually short of time when term papers are due, and you should be aware that using this book to learn search strategy and reference sources will take time for the first paper or two. However, once you have written two papers under the close guidance of this book, you will probably know what to do well enough to put the book aside, except for Appendix IV. More efficient use of the library will start to save you some time, and you can expect to see many of your former frustrations disappear. You will begin to look on future term paper assignments as a welcome chance to pursue your own interests and perhaps be truly creative. Using this book can be the difference between term papers that are a labor of love and papers that are just plain labor. It can also help your grades.

1 Choosing Your Topic

> "A great man will find a great subject, or which is the same thing, make a subject great."
> – Emerson, *Journals.*

How to Begin to Choose a Topic

There are two basic types of papers commonly required in psychology classes. Both start with a review of the literature — a search to trace down all research and theory on a particular topic. Once the paper is written, some assignments are complete, but others must be expanded into the design and performance of an experiment testing a hypothesis developed during the literature search. This book will prepare you to do literature searches. In Appendix IV we have provided references to handbooks which can help you in the actual writing of papers and in designing and conducting experiments.

If you can select your topic, choose a subject which really interests you. Such a topic will energize you, stir your imagination, and enliven your writing. Don't choose a topic just because it looks easy or because your professor seems to be interested in it.

For the sample topic in this book, let's say you have chosen to study the effect on viewers of television violence. As a television viewer yourself, you have seen violence in news and dramatic presentations and have thought about its possible effects on yourself and others. You are aware that it is a topic that has aroused a great deal of interest and controversy. You have observed that some stations either limit or exploit violence in their broadcasts, but you do not really

"I need some help with a paper on human emotion. Does the library have anything on rage?"

know if anyone has studied the effects of violence on the television audience.

Why Look for Authoritative Summaries?

You are a fledgling scholar in the subject and do not have an understanding of the scope of the subject and its various components. Also, you know from previous library searches that you are likely to come across unfamiliar technical terms. For those reasons it is important that you begin your search by looking for authoritative summaries of the topic, which should

1) Give you an overview of the topic;

2) Assist you in narrowing the scope of your topic;

3) Define commonly used technical terms;

4) Provide a bibliography of the "best" sources.

Where to Find Summaries

Summarizing discussions can be found in special encyclopedias, in textbooks, in books put on reserve by your instructor, and in other books your reference librarian can recommend. The best encyclopedia to use at the beginning of most psychology searches is the *International Encyclopedia of Psychiatry, Psychology, Psychoanalysis, & Neurology*, 12 volumes (New York: Van Nostrand Reinhold, 1977). Some 2,000 authorities contributed to this work, bringing together information about all aspects of mental health and mental disorders. Articles summarizing the work and theories of many individuals prominent in psychology are included, as are brief summaries of each contributor's area of study. The result is the most up-to-date comprehensive encyclopedia in psychology. Since volume 12 fully indexes the first 11 volumes which are alphabetically arranged by major topics, the index volume is the place to start your search. Some topics lacking major articles are accessible only through the listings in the index, and major topics in the alphabetical arrangement may have important aspects developed in articles scattered throughout the other volumes.

When searching any index you should not search just one or two headings. Do a thorough search under all headings you think may be related to your topic. For the topic of violence on television, you might think of headings like "Violence," "Television violence," and "Mass media." FIGURE 1.1 shows index entries from the *International Encyclopedia of Psychiatry, Psychology, Psychoanalysis, & Neurology*. Aspects of the topic are brought together in the index, as in the example of "Violence," and may be listed as subdivisions, as under "Television." "Mass media" has some especially promising subheadings such as "Antisocial newscasts" and "Mass media and violence." The Roman numerals are volume numbers, followed by page numbers. Notice how the information about violence on television is located in several places (e.g. volumes 7 and 11). The analyzing and gathering functions performed by the index provide a useful approach to the information in an encyclopedia.

Mass communication media. *See* Mass media
Mass contagion   III: 336
► Mass media   III: 216; VII: 35, 36, 37–39, 39–42;
    VIII: 309; X: 311; IX: 194, 362
  antisocial newscasts   VII: 36, 38
  impact of television   VII: 38
  prosocial values   VII: 36
  and violence   VII: 39–42
Mass persuasion   IX: 374
Mass psy̲c̲h̲.̲   ̲ ̲.̲ ̲.̲ ̲   ̲ ̲.̲ ̲ 56
M̲.̲ ̲ ̲ ̲ ̲ ̲ ̲ ̲ ̲ ̲ ̲ ̲ ̲ ̲ ̲ ̲ ̲ ̲ ̲.̲ ̲.̲.̲
    ..ephalon   III: 40,
Teleology   IX: 332; XI: 92–93, 270, 340
Telepathy   VIII: 184, 185, 186, 187, 188; XI: 67
► Television   I: 352, 353; II: 212; III: 353; V: 485;
    VII: 36, 38, 40; X: 311; XI: 93–97; VIII: 329
  antisocial content   I: 352
  educational   VII: 38
  family programming   VII: 40
  and psychiatry   XI: 93–97
  and social behavior   I: 353
  as a therapeutic tool   II: 212
  violence   VII: 36, 38; XI: 95
Temazepam   VIII: 346
Temperament   ̲ ̲ ̲I: 32; VI: 23, 24, 25
       ̲ ̲ ̲ ̲cial ̲ ̲ ̲   . 223, 334;
    VI: 113; VII: 179
Violence: Treatment   XI: 383–386
► Violence, violent behavior   I: 271, 346, 347,
    348, 351, 355, 356, 428, 433; II: 27, 28,
    70, 149, 412; V: 325; VI: 264, 275, 356,
    357; VII: 35, 36, 38, 40; VIII: 50, 51,
    430, 431; IX: 71, 72, 107, 307, 361, 362;
    X: 196, 288, 380, 433; XI: 95, 383
Viral encephalitis   VII: 196, 226, 462; VIII:

FIGURE 1.1 International Encyclopedia of Psychiatry, Psychology, Psychoanalysis & Neurology, 1977. Subject Index

The subheading "Mass media and violence" directs you to volume 7, pages 39–42. The article there explains several theories on the relationships between viewers and televised violence, and how the theories have changed and developed over time. The author of the article is Percy Tannenbaum. Authors of encyclopedia articles can generally be assumed to be authorities in their subject, so Tannenbaum will be a name to remember as you continue your research. You may look for reports of his research in periodical indexes and his books in the library catalog.

In addition to providing introductory information, encyclopedias can indicate to you whether research on your chosen topic will generate too much or too little information for you to use in your paper. For example, reading the vari-

---

actively ... participant rather ... relatively passive receiver.

Current TV industry practice tends to encourage the increased instigation of aggressive dispositions. This is not to imply that such practices are deliberate; quite the opposite is probably true. But some selection has to be made, and the tendency in any organization is for such patterns of selective treatment to become regularized over time. An important policy issue is thus who makes the selection and by what criteria, and to what degree those criteria can be informed by appropriate social psychological research.

BIBLIOGRAPHY

BANDURA, A. *Aggression: A social learning analysis.* Englewood Cliffs, N.J.: Prentice-Hall, 1973.

BERKOWITZ, L. The frustration-aggression hypothesis revised. In L. Berkowitz (Ed.), *Roots of aggression: A re-examination of the frustration-aggression hypothesis.* New York: Atherton Press, 1969.

CATER, D., and STRICKLAND, S. *TV violence and the child: The evolution and fate of the surgeon general's report.* New York: Russell Sage Foundation, 1975.

FESHBACH, S., and SINGER, R. *Television and aggression.* San Francisco: Jossey-Bass, 1971.

HOWITT, D., and CUMBERBATCH, G. *Mass media violence and society.* London: Paul Elek, 1975.

TANNENBAUM, P. H., and ZILLMAN, D. Emotional arousal in the facilitation of aggression through communication. In L. Berkowitz (Ed.), *Advances in experimental social psychology* (Vol. 9). New York: Academic Press, 1975.

Television and growing up: The impact of televised violence. Report to the Surgeon General of the United States Public Health Service from the Surgeon General's Scientific Advisory Committee on Television and Social Behavior. Washington: Government Printing Office, 1971.

PERCY H. TANNENBAUM

FIGURE 1.2. "Mass media and violence" In International Encyclopedia of Psychiatry, Psychology, Psychoanalysis & Neurology, 1977. Vol. 7, p. 39–42.

ous articles on television and violence in the *International Encyclopedia of Psychiatry, Psychology, Psychoanalysis, & Neurology* tells you enough about the subject to make you realize that it is probably too broad to be adequately discussed in a typical research paper. However, one aspect of the topic, antisocial newscasts, strikes you as an interesting and workable topic for your paper, and it is this topic on which you decide to focus.

To keep the scope of research manageable, it is helpful to state precisely the question you want to answer, such as "Does violence in television newscasts have some effect on the behavior or attitudes of viewers?" You will sometimes find a research topic stated as a "null hypothesis," which is a statement assuming that certain factors have no effect on the subjects; restating our question as a null hypothesis would result in the statement "Violence in television newscasts has no effect on the behavior or attitudes of viewers." With a null hypothesis, the researcher tries to objectively assume that there is no effect, then studies the research and statistics to see if there really is some effect. Even after you have clearly stated your research topic, however, you should be prepared to further refine the topic as you continue your research. For example, you are starting your research by studying the group of subjects "television viewers," but as you review more of the research, you may find that you want to narrow your group of subjects to viewers who are adults, children, teen-age boys, or prison inmates. Or perhaps you will find enough information to narrow the kind of violence studied to violence in street crime or violence in war and terrorist activities.

Even though you have narrowed the scope of your paper, you will need to become familiar with some of the general background material related to your topic. Here, too, encyclopedias are useful as an important source of bibliographies. FIGURE 1.2 shows a bibliography of works basic to the understanding of mass media and violence which Tannenbaum has included at the end of his article. Of these, the books by S. Feshbach and D. Howitt and the Surgeon General's *Report* appear to be most useful for your topic.

Another encyclopedia to consult for a general summary of a topic is the *International Encyclopedia of the Social Sciences*, 18 Volumes (New York: Macmillan, 1968). Typically, you should use the index to gather scattered information about prominent individuals, bibliographies, and articles on major concepts, theories, and methods in psychology and the other social sciences.

Comparison of the index entries for "Television" in the two encyclopedias demonstrates the difference in coverage (FIGURE 1.3). While the *International Encyclopedia of the Social Sciences* is older, which limits its value, it can provide a valuable historical perspective on some topics and can give good coverage on theories developed prior to 1968. The *International Encyclopedia of the Social Sciences* shows the relationship of television to a wide range of subjects. The *International Encyclopedia of Psychiatry, Psychology, Psychoanalysis, & Neurology* more closely details the psycho-

---

Television   I: 352, 353; II: 212; III: 353; V: 485;
   VII: 36, 38, 40; X: 311; XI: 93–97; VIII: 329
   antisocial content   I: 352
   educational   VII: 38
   family programming   VII: 40
   and psychiatry   XI: 93–97
   and social behavior   I: 353
   as a therapeutic tool   II: 212
   violence   VII: 36, 38; XI: 95

Television
   adult education 1:102
   advertising research 1:110
   audiences 3:71, 72, 74, 75, 77
   communication, mass 3:47, 49, 50,
      63, 87, 88
   communication, political 3:94
   control and public policy 3:58, 59
   film 5:426, 428, 430
   regulation of industry 13:395
   socialization: psychological aspects
      14:543
   space, outer: social and psychological aspects 15:93

FIGURE 1.3. Comparison of index entries: (top) International Encyclopedia of Psychiatry, Psychology, Psychoanalysis, & Neurology compared to (bottom) International Encyclopedia of the Social Sciences.

---

logical aspects of television.

While the *International Encyclopedia of Psychiatry, Psychology, Psychoanalysis, & Neurology* and the *International Encyclopedia of the Social Sciences* are basic sources which should be consulted at the beginning of a search for information within the general field of psychology, there are other more specialized encyclopedias useful for study in more limited areas of psychology, such as the *Encyclopedia of Human Behavior*, 2 volumes (Garden City, NY: Doubleday, 1970). It is not necessary to remember the titles of all psychology reference sources. Instead, you should consult one or more of the following sources to identify appropriate titles:

1) Appendix IV of this book, "Basic reference sources for psychology courses;"

2) Chapter 7 of this book, "Using guides to the literature of psychology;"

3) Your reference librarian.

Why Ask Your Reference Librarian?

Maybe encyclopedias, textbooks, and reserve books will all fail to supply the needed summaries. This does not mean you should change topics without further research. First ask your reference librarian for help. A reference librarian's job is to help students and faculty use the library effectively, but she or he is not a mind reader. If you have a problem, go to the Reference Desk, ask your question as precisely as you can, and tell the librarian where you have already looked. The librarian may lead you to encyclopedias you never heard of or may show you particular subject headings in the card catalog. However, after some searching, the librarian may conclude that the library does not have the summary discussions you need. In fact, she or he may recommend that you change your topic because the library's resources seem to be too limited. It is better to change a dead-end topic early, before you have invested too much time in it.

Your professor is also a valuable resource person who can suggest materials on a given topic.

Summary

To conclude this chapter, we can summarize your search up to this point as follows:

1) Begin your search by finding a good overview of the topic. For most psychology topics, encyclopedias such as *International Encyclopedia of Psychiatry, Psychology, Psychoanalysis, & Neurology* and *International Encyclopedia of the Social Sciences* are good sources for background material.

2) The encyclopedia index brings together various aspects of your topic. The information in the encyclopedia articles can help you determine whether you should narrow or broaden the scope of your topic.

3) When you have determined the scope of your research topic, state it as a question, a statement, or a null hypothesis, to help you stay on the subject as you continue your research.

4) The bibliographies following encyclopedia articles provide more sources to consult.

5) If these encyclopedias do not cover your topic well enough, consult Appendix IV for more specialized encyclopedias, or ask your reference librarian for help.

2 Communicating with the Card Catalog

"We tie knots and bind up words in double meanings, and then try to untie them."
— Seneca, *Epistulae ad Lucillium.*

Limitations and Difficulties of the Card Catalog

You may think of the card catalog as the most important single reference source in the library, but are you aware of its limitations? It indexes only the *general* subjects of *books*. It does not index parts of most books, nor does it provide access to periodical articles. In many libraries the card catalog does not include government documents. And it does not give much help in evaluating the books it lists.

A card catalog is usually simple to use if you need a particular book and know its author or title. You simply look up the author or title and copy down its call number. The big difficulty with the card catalog comes when you try to find what books the library has on a particular subject. Then you must cope with the special language of subject headings, which is significantly different from spoken English.

Using What You Already Know

There are two main ways to identify the proper subject headings for your topic. One way is to use the subject tracings on catalog cards. Earlier in this text we searched the encyclopedias and found a reference to S. Feshbach's *Television and Aggression*. Naturally, you would go to the card catalog to see if your library has it. When you look it up, note the subject tracing "Violence in television" printed at the bottom of the card (FIGURE 2.1), and then look for other books under that same subject heading.

There are problems, however, with this approach. First of all, the Feshbach book was selected as one which could give you background in television and aggression, but it may or may not be helpful with "violence in television news." Therefore, the headings assigned to this book may not lead you to other books that focus precisely on the aspects you

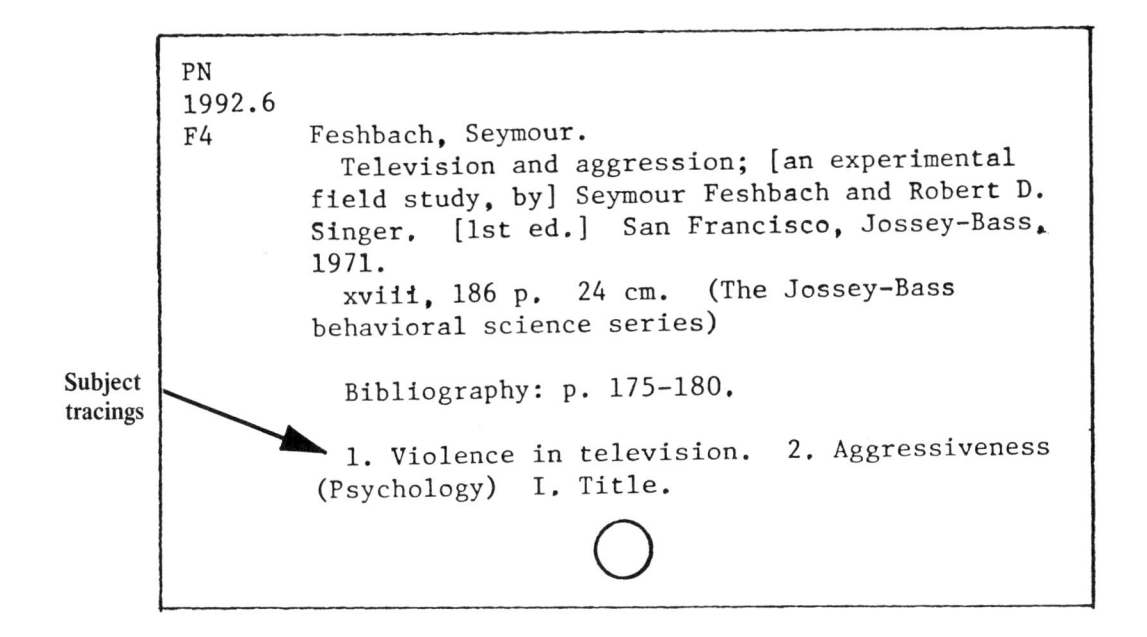

```
PN
1992.6
F4      Feshbach, Seymour.
            Television and aggression; [an experimental
        field study, by] Seymour Feshbach and Robert D.
        Singer. [1st ed.] San Francisco, Jossey-Bass,
        1971.
            xviii, 186 p.  24 cm.  (The Jossey-Bass
        behavioral science series)

            Bibliography: p. 175-180.

Subject
tracings ──▶  1. Violence in television.  2. Aggressiveness
        (Psychology)  I. Title.
```

FIGURE 2.1. Catalog card illustrating subject tracing.

need. Even if the book seems perfect, there are probably additional titles under related headings that you would find useful. Another problem is that some libraries do not have the subject tracings at the bottom of all cards. There is also the possibility that your library does not have the books listed in the encyclopedia bibliography.

The most effective way to use the card catalog is to determine several related subject headings before you start looking for specific titles. You can select the headings by using a guide to the subject catalog.

The Language of Subject Headings

Most college and university libraries do not invent their own subject headings, but use whatever headings are assigned to books by the Library of Congress, the nation's largest library. The Library of Congress publishes a guide, the *Library of Congress Subject Headings*, 9th ed., (Washington: Library of Congress, 1980), which lists subject headings along with extensive cross references. There are two formats available: one consists of two big, red volumes accompanied

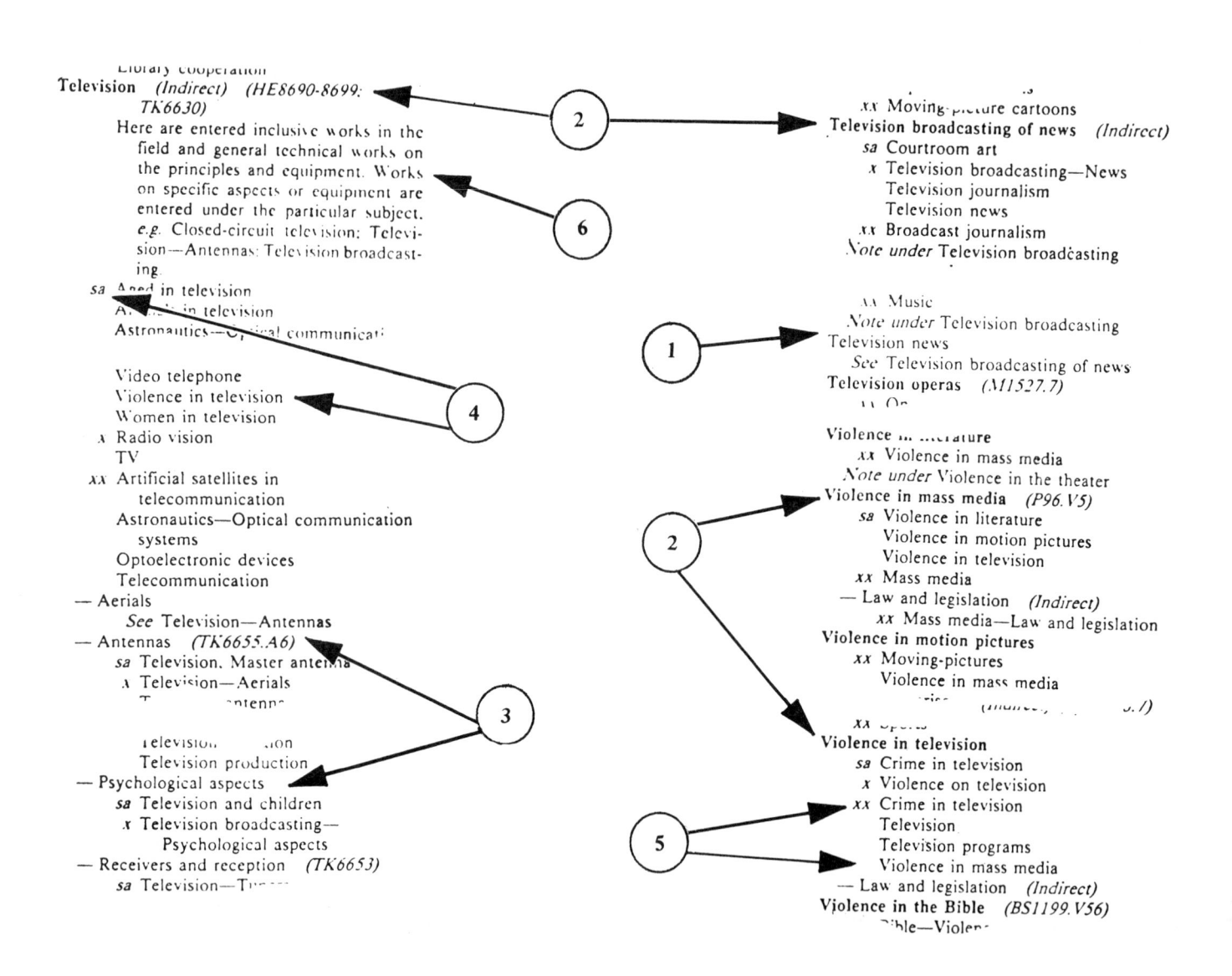

```
Library cooperation
Television  (Indirect)  (HE8690-8699;
      TK6630)
    Here are entered inclusive works in the
    field and general technical works on
    the principles and equipment. Works
    on specific aspects or equipment are
    entered under the particular subject.
    e.g. Closed-circuit television; Televi-
    sion—Antennas; Television broadcast-
    ing.
  sa Aged in television
     A.... in television
     Astronautics—Optical communicati
     
     Video telephone
     Violence in television
     Women in television
   x Radio vision
     TV
  xx Artificial satellites in
       telecommunication
     Astronautics—Optical communication
       systems
     Optoelectronic devices
     Telecommunication
  — Aerials
      See Television—Antennas
  — Antennas  (TK6655.A6)
     sa Television, Master antenna
      x Television—Aerials
      
     Television
     Television production
  — Psychological aspects
     sa Television and children
      x Television broadcasting—
          Psychological aspects
  — Receivers and reception  (TK6653)
     sa Television—T
```

```
  xx Moving-picture cartoons
Television broadcasting of news  (Indirect)
  sa Courtroom art
   x Television broadcasting—News
     Television journalism
     Television news
  xx Broadcast journalism
  Note under Television broadcasting

  xx Music
  Note under Television broadcasting
Television news
     See Television broadcasting of news
Television operas  (M1527.7)
  
Violence in literature
  xx Violence in mass media
  Note under Violence in the theater
Violence in mass media  (P96.V5)
  sa Violence in literature
     Violence in motion pictures
     Violence in television
  xx Mass media
  — Law and legislation  (Indirect)
     xx Mass media—Law and legislation
Violence in motion pictures
  xx Moving-pictures
     Violence in mass media

  xx Opera
Violence in television
  sa Crime in television
   x Violence on television
  xx Crime in television
     Television
     Television programs
     Violence in mass media
  — Law and legislation  (Indirect)
Violence in the Bible  (BS1199.V56)
     Bible—Violen
```

FIGURE 2.2. Library of Congress Subject Headings

by paperback supplements, and the other is a set of microfiche which is issued quarterly in revised cumulations. In either format, *Library of Congress Subject Headings* is essential for effective searching in the subject catalog.

Look in the *Library of Congress Subject Headings* under terms you think might apply to your topic. Although the vocabulary used in the list is arbitrary and you might not think of the exact words used there, usually you will find cross references to lead you to the established terms. For instance, if you look up "Television news" in the list, you will be told to "*see* Television broadcasting of news." FIGURE 2.2 demonstrates the layout of the *Library of Congress Subject Headings*. Many libraries put "see" and "see also" cards in their catalogs as cross references, but they cannot always keep up with the large number of additions and changes in headings. If you don.t find the *Library of Congress Subject Headings* volumes or microfiche near the card catalog, ask a reference librarian to get them for you. The librarian can show you how to use them, or there might be a sign posted with instructions for their use. If you can find the books but no instructions, studying FIGURE 2.2 should get you started.

It appears from a study of the *Library of Congress Subject Headings* that the following headings might be useful for your topic "violence in television news and its effects on viewers":

---

1. "see" refers you from a heading which is not authorized for use in the catalog.

2. Headings in bold print are authorized for use.

3. Dashes indicate subdivisions. Under "Television" a useful subdivison is "Psychological aspects."

4. "sa" stands for "see also" and refers to one or more related headings. The reference most relevant to our topic is "Violence in television." The "sa" references are often more specific than the bold-face heading above them.

5. "xx" also stands for "see also" but directs you to a somewhat broader related subject. If you do not find enough material under specific subjects, you may have to check under slightly broader ones.

6. Scope note, explaining the coverage of the heading, and suggesting related headings.

Television — Psychological aspects
Television broadcasting of news
Violence in mass media
Violence in television

Since there will seldom be a single heading which covers all aspects of a topic, it is important to select several headings from the list and check all of them to see which ones are most useful.

Choosing the Best Books

When you have chosen your subject headings and located the cards in the catalog, you will need to select the few "best books" under those headings. If there are many books under the headings you have selected, you might want to try to choose useful ones without looking at all of them. There is no certain way to determine from the cards which books are best, but there is information on the cards that can help eliminate those which most likely will not be useful for your topic. FIGURE 2.3 shows several cards which are filed under the headings selected from the *Library of Congress Subject Headings*. The cards illustrate the use of the following criteria in making judgements about which books to skip:

1) Date of publication. The most recent books are generally more desirable because their authors have had access to more accumulated knowledge. The summarizing encyclopedia article covered much research up to the mid-1970s, so you would be more interested in materials after that time.

2) Author's authority. You may instantly recognize certain authors as authorities; perhaps your professor put some of their writings on reserve or you remember their names from bibliographies you have already used.

3) The subject tracings and title. These may tell more about the scope of the book. If you are interested only in adult reactions to television news violence, you would probably reject the book *Television and Children*.

4) Bibliographic note. A book with a bibliography will generally be more useful and scholarly than one without a bibliography.

5) Publisher's reputation. Major university presses and better-known independent publishers can be trusted to publish reliable books in psychology.

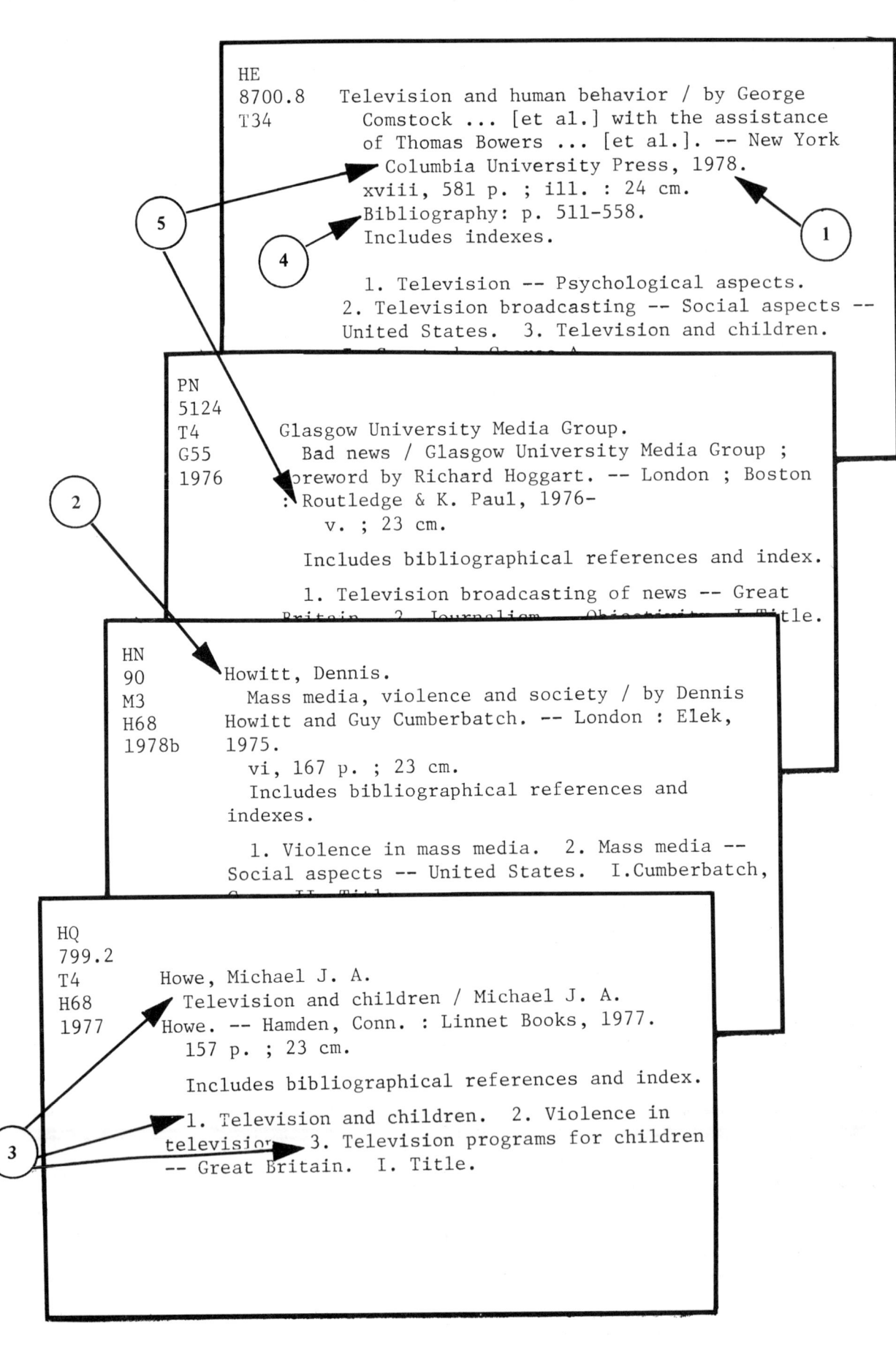

```
HE
8700.8    Television and human behavior / by George
T34         Comstock ... [et al.] with the assistance
            of Thomas Bowers ... [et al.]. -- New York
          : Columbia University Press, 1978.
            xviii, 581 p. ; ill. : 24 cm.
            Bibliography: p. 511-558.
            Includes indexes.

            1. Television -- Psychological aspects.
            2. Television broadcasting -- Social aspects --
            United States.  3. Television and children.
```

```
PN
5124
T4
G55       Glasgow University Media Group.
1976        Bad news / Glasgow University Media Group ;
            foreword by Richard Hoggart. -- London ; Boston
          : Routledge & K. Paul, 1976-
             v. ; 23 cm.

            Includes bibliographical references and index.

            1. Television broadcasting of news -- Great
```

```
HN
90
M3        Howitt, Dennis.
H68         Mass media, violence and society / by Dennis
1978b     Howitt and Guy Cumberbatch. -- London : Elek,
          1975.
            vi, 167 p. ; 23 cm.
            Includes bibliographical references and
          indexes.

            1. Violence in mass media.  2. Mass media --
          Social aspects -- United States.  I. Cumberbatch,
```

```
HQ
799.2
T4        Howe, Michael J. A.
H68         Television and children / Michael J. A.
1977      Howe. -- Hamden, Conn. : Linnet Books, 1977.
            157 p. ; 23 cm.

            Includes bibliographical references and index.

            1. Television and children.  2. Violence in
          television.  3. Television programs for children
          -- Great Britain.  I. Title.
```

FIGURE 2.3. Library of Congress catalog cards. Numbers explained in text.

Summary

1. The card catalog is limited because it indexes the *general* subject of *books* only, and it does not evaluate them.

2. The language of subject headings used in the card catalog is complex and arbitrary. The best guide to such headings is the *Library of Congress Subject Headings*. A copy published as a set of two red volumes with paperback supplements or as a set of microfiche is usually shelved near the card catalog.

3. Use headings that have been applied to books about which you already know.

4. Search in the *Subject Headings* list for the several headings which best represent or encompass your topic.

5. If a heading produces insufficient material, use a more general heading.

6. You can tentatively evaluate a book on the basis of its catalog card by noting the following: date of publication, author's authority, title and other subject headings, publisher's reputation, and bibliographic note.

3 Reviews of the Literature: *Annual Review of Psychology*

> "To live effectively is to live with adequate information."
> — Norbert Wiener, *The Human Use of Human Beings*

For two reasons, books and encyclopedias do not often reflect the current status of a specific topic, nor will they indicate the directions in which current research is headed. First, the writing and publishing of a book is a complicated process that can take as many as three years to complete. Second, the type of sources you have looked at so far were written to present the factual and conceptual scope of a broad subject, such as television violence. These sources do not focus on the latest findings in a specific research area, such as the effects of the violence in television news broadcasts on adult behavior.

To obtain a perspective on the current status of an area of research and to get the latest information, two types of sources should be used: review serials and research reports. We will deal with review serials here and will cover access to research reports in Chapters 4 and 5.

Review Serials

Review serials may be defined as publications that come out in parts, have a common title, and contain a number of articles or chapters that give a critical analysis of recent developments and research in a particular area. They usually limit discussion to the one or two years previous to publication. These serials are published in a variety of formats and with various frequencies. As a result, libraries handle review serials in a number of different ways. Monthly or quarterly review serials may be shelved as part of a separate journal collection in some libraries. Annual or biennial review serials might be shelved in the Reference Department or with books on the subject. Still others are irregular in their publication schedule and may be shelved in any of the locations mentioned.

Choosing a Review Serial

Since it is impossible for you to know about all of the review serials that exist, you will need help in identifying appropriate titles. Three possibilities are listed below:

1) Consult Appendix IV of this guide for other general psychology review serials, and also check the appropriate subject sections of this Appendix. For example, the section on abnormal psychology cites seven review serials, including *Year Book of Psychiatry and Applied Mental Health*. However, since the list in Appendix IV will no doubt be outdated fairly quickly, you will want to try the other methods listed below as well.

2) Consult the card catalog of your library under the broad subject heading into which your topic fits and look for the subdivisions "Periodicals" and "Annuals." This can be a tricky matter and usually requires searching under more headings than you would initially think to check. For example, while "psychology is the obvious heading for your topic, other possible subjects are "psychiatry," and even "sociology," since there may be review serials in those areas which contain relevant articles. Another problem with using the card catalog is that some libraries don't list periodicals in the card catalog.

3) Ask your librarian or professor to suggest possible review serials.

Once you have identified the appropriate title(s), you will need to determine whether your library has them. You may have to check the card catalog and/or a periodicals list or a serials catalog. In any case you will search under the title of the serial, and by all means ask the librarian for help if you need it. Look at the section of Appendix IV which lists the review serials in psychology. Once you have determined that your library has them and where they are shelved, you can consult them for articles. Remember, you are only interested in the material that is more current than the sources you have already consulted. Because it often takes as long as two or three years to get a book published, you should begin your search with issues of review serials published two or three years *before publication* of the recent relevant texts you used. In this case, the most useful sources are Feshbach (1971), the Surgeon General's Report (1971) and Howitt (1975). Therefore, you should confine your search to the period 1970 to the present.

How to Use the Annual Review of Psychology

The *Annual Review of Psychology* (Stanford, CA: Annual Reviews, 1950--) is an excellent source for most

→ SOCIAL PSYCHOLOGY
    Attitudes and Opinions — C. A. Kiesler, P. A. Munson — 26:415–55
    The Social Psychology of Small Groups:
      Cooperative and Mixed-Motive Interaction — J. H. Davis, P. R. Laughlin, S. S. Komorita — 27:501–41
→   Effects of Mass Media — R. M. Liebert, N. S. Schwartzberg — 28:141–73
    Interpersonal Attraction and Relationships — T. L. Huston, G. Levinger — 29:115–56
    Environmental Psychology — D. Stokols — 29:253–95
    Attitudes and Opinions — A. H. Eagly, S. Himmelfarb — 29:517–54
    What's Cultural About Cross-Cultural Cognitive Psychology? — Laboratory of Comparative Human Cognition — 30:145–72
    The Psychology of Group Processes — A. Zander — 30:417–51

SPECIAL TOPICS
    The Psychology of Women—Selected Topics — M. T. S. Mednick, H. J. Weissman — 26:1–18
    Drug Use and Abuse — W. H. McGlothlin — 26:45–64
    Psychology and the Law: An Overture — J. L. Tapp — 27:359–404
    Program Evaluation — R. Perloff, E. Perloff, E. Sussna — 27:569–94
    Psychological and Physiological Mechanisms of Pain — J. C. Liebeskind, L. A. Paul — 28:41–60
    Psychological Perspectives on Death — R. Kastenbaum, P. T. Costa Jr. — 28:225–49
    Twenty Years of Experimental Gaming: Critique, Synthesis, and Suggestions for the Future — D. G. Pruitt, M. J. Kimmel — 28:363–92
    Nutrition, Malnutrition, and Behavior — J. Brožek — 29:157–77
    Biofeedback and Visceral Learning — N. E. Miller — 29:373–404
    Some Origins of Psychology As Science — C. G. Mueller — 30:9–29
    Facial Expressions of Emotion — P. Ekman, H. Oster — 30:527–54

VISION
    See RECEPTOR PROCESSES

FIGURE 3.1. Cumulative list of chapter titles, Annual Review of Psychology, v. 30, p. 693.

---

topics in psychology and will serve as an example in explaining the use of review serials. Review serials usually have an index to authors cited in the review articles, as well as some kind of subject index. Besides an index of cited authors and a subject index for each volume, the *Annual Review of Psychology* has a five-year cumulative list of review chapter titles, which serves as another form of subject index. FIGURE 3.1 shows a section of the cumulative list of chapter titles for volumes 26–30 (1975–1979) of the *Annual Review of Psychology*. The chapter titles are arranged in broad categories such as Cognitive Processes, Developmental Psychology, and so on. In FIGURE 3.1 it is easy to identify one article that may be relevant. But is is important not to rely exclusively on these title lists. Since you are interested in specific information on the effects of television news violence, you should use the second type of subject approach, the individual volume indexes.

FIGURE 3.2 illustrates the usefulness of the subject index in pinpointing specific information, with two listings for television violence. FIGURE 3.3 shows part of the review article pointed to by the index and a few of the references cited by the author of the review. These citations are one of the most important reasons why you should search for a review serial.

If you have done a thorough and thoughtful job to this

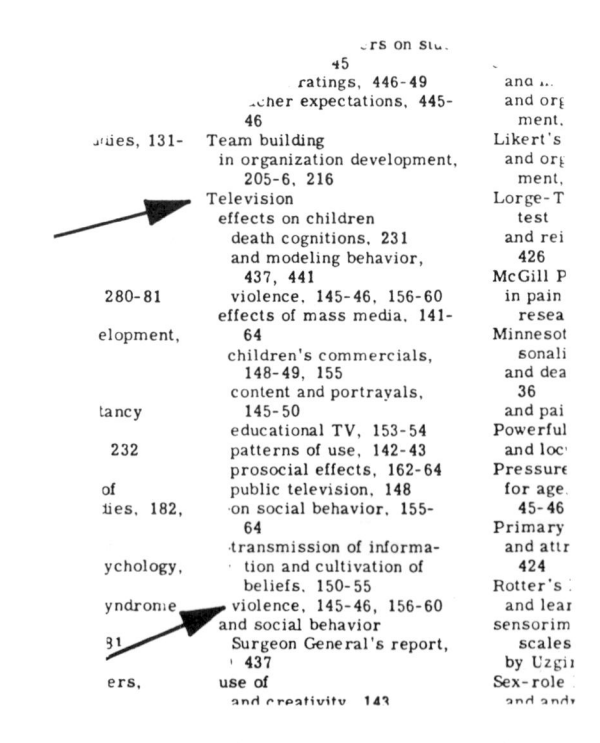

    ...rs on stu.
      45
    ratings, 446-49
    ..cher expectations, 445-46
..dies, 131- Team building
      in organization development, 205-6, 216
→ Television
    effects on children
      death cognitions, 231
      and modeling behavior, 437, 441
280-81   violence, 145-46, 156-60
    effects of mass media, 141-64
elopment, children's commercials, 148-49, 155
    content and portrayals, 145-50
tancy   educational TV, 153-54
232   patterns of use, 142-43
    prosocial effects, 162-64
of   public television, 148
ties, 182, on social behavior, 155-64
    transmission of information and cultivation of
ychology, beliefs, 150-55
yndrome→ violence, 145-46, 156-60
    and social behavior
31   Surgeon General's report, 437
ers, use of
    and creativity, 143

FIGURE 3.2. Annual Review of Psychology, vol. 28. Subject index, p. 496.

point, you will be as knowledgeable about the subject and its bibliography as any but the most expert research worker in the field. You will know the dimensions of the topic and the fundamental problems still unresolved; you will know who the major contributors are and what they have written. Now you are ready to plunge into the ocean of recent research on the effects on viewers of the depiction of violence in television news broadcasts.

---

st̮.
electric s̮. ̮ imitative ag̮.
white viewers. ̮. ̮as not diminished by hav̮.̮
by the black victim wi̮.. ̮ ̮lm. On the other hand, Milgram & Sho̮..
performed a series of field experiments which showed that a single exposure to .
antisocial behavior of one dispirited protagonist did not lead to imitation in adults. More seductive acts of antisocial behavior may nonetheless induce imitation in adults, as correlational studies on imitation of the criminal plots of such films as *The Doomsday Flight* seem to suggest (164).

➤ DISINHIBITION OF AGGRESSION: CORRELATIONAL STUDIES Five major correlational studies appear in the Surgeon General's report, and all of them found some association between TV violence viewing and aggressiveness. McIntyre & Teevan (185) found a significant relationship between the amount of violence in a youngster's favorite TV programs and the amount of aggressiveness he or she displayed on five scales of deviance (e.g. petty delinquency) and three measures of approval of violence among 2300 junior and senior high school boys and girls in a sample that was about 15% black and covered the gamut of SES backgrounds. Robinson & Bachman (223) found that adolescent boys high in TV violence viewing were more likely than low TV violence viewers to have gotten into a serious fight at school or work, hurt someone badly enough to need bandages, or to have ̮̮ipated in a gang fight. Studying almost 1000 fourth, fifth, and sixth grade boys
̮̮minick & Greenberg (68) foun̮ ̮̮ater the level of exposure
̮̮. the more the ̮¹ ̮̮nce, to suggest it
̮d t̮ ̮ ̮nd, Atkin
̮ ̮ol

cation, ed. F. G. Kline, P. J. Tichenon, pp. 95-120. Beverly Hills: Sage. 320 pp.
➤ 35. Chaffee, S. H. 1972. Television and adolescent aggressiveness (overview). In *Television and Social Behavior, Vol. 3: Television and Adolescent Aggressiveness*, ed. G. A. Comstock, E. A. Rubinstein, pp. 1-34. Washington DC: GPO. 435 pp.
36. Chaffee, S. H., Becker, L. B. 1974. *Impact of Watergate on the Young Voter.* Presented at Central States Speech Assoc., Milwaukee, Wisc.
37. Chaffee, S. H., Izcaray, F. 1975. *Models of Mass Communication for a Media-*
̮̮̮̮ ̮̮̮̮̮̮̮̮ ̮̮̮̮̮̮̮ ̮̮̮̮̮̮̮̮̮ ̮̮

➤ 185. McIntyre, J. J., Teevan, J. J. Jr. 1972. Television violence and deviant behavior. See Ref. 35, pp. 383-435
186. McLeod, J. M., Atkin, C. K., Chaffee, S. H. 1972. Adolescents, parents and television use: self-report and other-report measures from the Wisconsin sample. See Ref. 35, pp. 239-313
187. McLeod, J. M., Becker, L. B. 1974. Testing the validity of gratification measures through political effects analysis. See Ref. 108, pp. 137-64
188. McLeod, J. M., Becker, L. B., Byrnes, J. E. 1974. Another look at the agenda-setting function of the press. *Commun. Res.* 1:131-66
189. McLeod, J. M., Brown, J. D., Becker,

FIGURE 3.3. "Effects of mass media" in Annual Review of Psychology, vol. 28, p. 157-170.

Summary

1. Review serials are important sources of current information on a topic and should be used as a link between books and encyclopedias and research reports.

2. Identification of the appropriate review serials can be difficult. You should consult Appendix IV of this guide, check the card catalog, or ask your librarian or professor.

3. Study the relevant material carefully and make notes of the information, key terms, and significant citations.

4 The Subject Approach and Computer Searching:
Social Sciences Index, Psychological Abstracts, Sociological Abstracts, **and "Permuterm Index"** of *Social Sciences Citation Index*

> "Every question in literature, religion, politics, social science, political economy, and in many other lines of human progress, finds its latest and freshest interpretations in the current periodicals. No one can thoroughly investigate any of these questions without knowing what the periodicals have said and are saying concerning them."
> — William Frederick Poole, Preface, *Poole's Index to Periodical Literature*

By this time, the preliminary stages of your research have been completed. You have consulted the appropriate encyclopedias to get an overview of your topic and have looked up some of the key sources listed in them in the card catalog. You have also used the card catalog to find other books on your topic and looked at these as well as the ones cited in the encyclopedias. In addition, you have read a review article from the *Annual Review of Psychology* or another review journal which indicates the state of knowledge about your topic at the time the review article was written, what work has been done, and what conclusions have been reached. The review article has also cited several relevant books and articles which you have noted.

Now you are ready to start searching for reports of original research which will update the information you have gathered thus far and focus more directly on your specific topic. For this final step in your search there are two basic approaches: the subject approach and the author approach. We will explain the first approach here and the second in Chapter 5.

Periodical Indexes

Maybe you had to write a paper early in your college career, and when it came time to find periodical articles, you turned to the *Readers' Guide* because that was the only periodical index you knew. *Readers' Guide* covers mostly popular magazines, however, which are inappropriate sources of information for a psychology paper. On the other hand, another student or your professor may have mentioned that you should use *Psychological Abstracts* (Washington, DC: American Psychological Association, 1927–) because it is generally the single best periodical index for psychological literature. Your library might not have it, though, and in some cases another index might be more appropriate.

No single index covers *all* the periodicals used in psychological research. Each index covers a different group, though there is some overlap, and a thorough search should include the use of several indexes. Indexes also use a variety of indexing techniques, and searching through several indexes can increase your chances of finding relevant articles. There are many — in fact, hundreds — of different indexes to periodical articles from which to choose, but few libraries have all of the indexes. The main part of this chapter will deal with four indexes to the psychological literature: 1) *Social Sciences Index*, 2) *Psychological Abstracts*, 3) *Sociological Abstracts*, and 4) the "Permuterm Index" of *Social Sciences Citation Index*. Later in this chapter we will say something about the choice of an appropriate index for a particular search.

The most efficient way to use any periodical index is to start with the most recent issues of the index and work your way back through older issues. When you start encountering the articles you had noted from your work with review serials, you will have searched backward far enough. Computers can also be used in the search process, as we will explain at the end of this chapter.

Social Sciences Index

Social Sciences Index (NY: Wilson, 1974–) is a companion to *Readers' Guide*. It is published by the same company and has the same general format. *Social Sciences Index* covers some 260 English language periodicals, about 35 of which are in psychology — only a fraction of the literature as compared to the 900 periodicals indexed by *Psychological Abstracts*. However, *Social Sciences Index* has several advantages: the journals it indexes are among the most important and therefore likely to be available in most college and university libraries; its interdisciplinary coverage of all social sciences may be helpful when your topic borders on sociology, economics, or other social sciences; and it is somewhat easier to use than *Psychological Abstracts*. For these reasons, you may prefer to begin your search with *Social Sciences Index* and then go on to *Psychological Abstracts* if more references are necessary.

Social Sciences Index uses standardized subject terms and includes cross-references to refer you to the correct ("see") and related ("see also") terms. For example, in the 1980–1981 issue there is a reference "Television news, see Television programs — News programs" and a reference "Television programs — Psychological aspects, see also Violence in television" (FIGURE 4.1). As you look through *Social Sciences Index*, you should jot down the headings which appear to be relevant to your topic to make sure you look them all up as your search progresses.

Psychological Abstracts . . . What Is It?

Unlike *Readers' Guide* and *Social Sciences Index*, *Psychological Abstracts* is more than just a periodical index. It might more properly be called an information resources directory. *Psychological Abstracts* indexes approximately 900 journals in 35 languages, with a total of 25 to 30,000 abstracts a year. Until 1980, references to books and dissertations were included, but since 1980, books are no longer indexed and dissertations are included only in the computerized version of *Psychological Abstracts*. The subjects included range over all the areas of psychological research and include such related disciplines as psychiatry, sociology, anthropology, and education.

The basic component of *Psychological Abstracts* is an abstract, a summary statement of the content of a document (see FIGURE 4.2). The first element of each abstract entry is the assigned abstract number. This is followed by all of the bibliographic information you normally associate with a citation or bibliographic reference: author(s), title of the article, title of the journal in which it appeared, volume, pages, and date. In addition, two other important pieces of

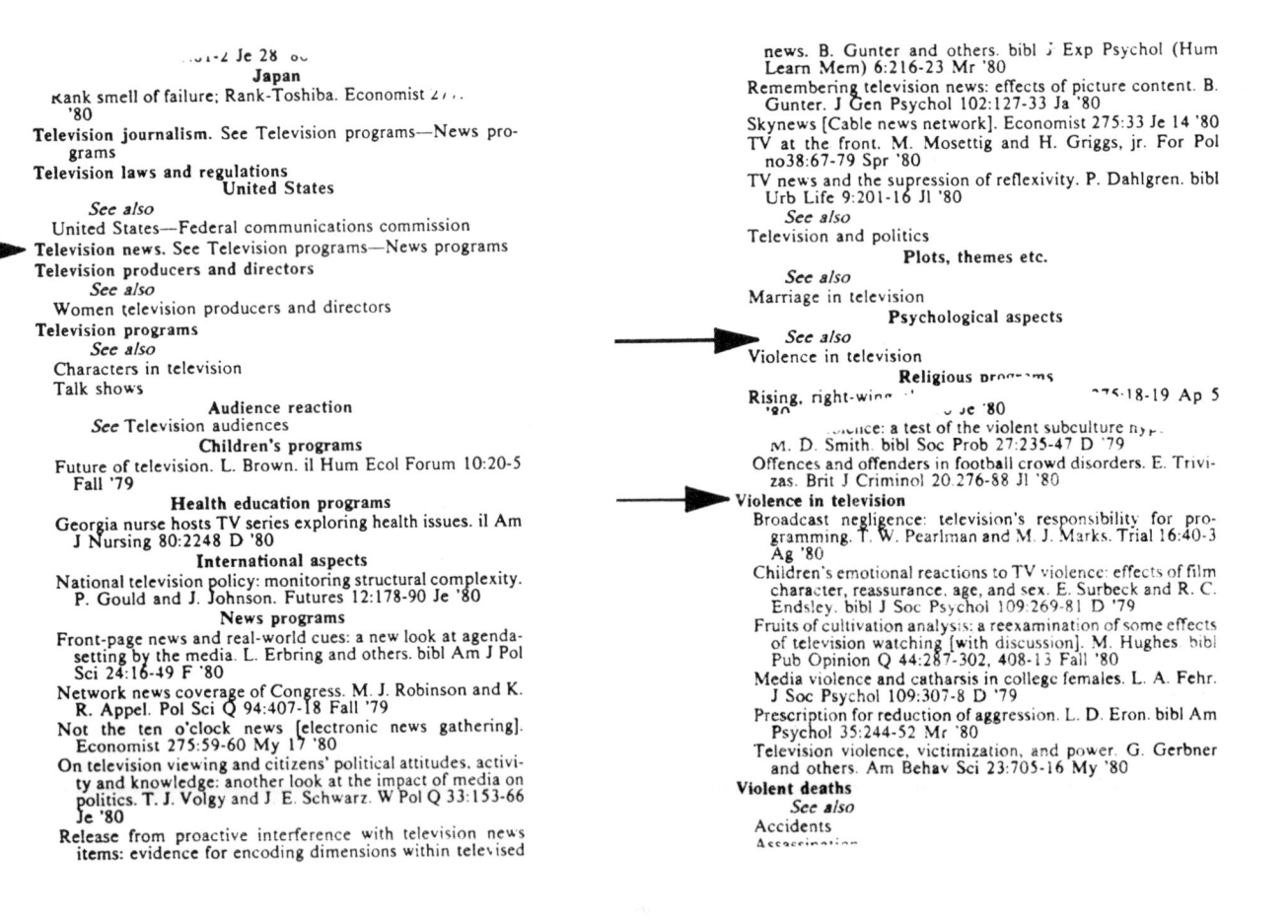

FIGURE 4.1 Social Sciences Index, April 1980-March 1981.

information are given: 1) Following the author's name is the institutional affiliation of the senior author. This enables users of *Psychological Abstracts* to communicate directly with authors in whose work they are interested. 2) Articles in foreign languages are indicated by placing brackets around the translated title and noting the original language in parentheses. If the primary publication includes a summary in a language other than that of the article, this information is noted at the end of the abstract. Certain abbreviations which appear frequently in psychology literature are used in the abstracts and are explained at the beginning of each issue of *Psychological Abstracts*.

The abstracts included in *Psychological Abstracts* are arranged in 16 broad subject categories which are further subdivided into more specific topics (see FIGURE 4.3). As each monthly issue is published, you can keep abreast of the developments in your areas of interest by scanning the abstracts in the relevant categories.

The subject headings used to index *Psychological Abstracts* are taken from a list called the *Thesaurus of Psychological Index Terms*, 3d ed. (Washington, DC: American Psychological Association, 1982). Most libraries shelve this right next to *Psychological Abstracts*, because it is a very useful book to check before beginning your search, just as the *Library of Congress Subject Headings* is useful for effective searching in the card catalog. There are two parts to this thesaurus, a "Relationship Section" and a "Rotated Alphabetical Terms Section." The "Relationship Section" (FIGURE 4.4) shows you what terms can be looked up in the *Psychological Abstracts* subject indexes and what related, broader, and narrower terms might also be of interest. The "Rotated Alphabetical Terms Section" arranges all significant words in the subject headings in alphabetical order (see FIGURE 4.5). Thus, whether you think of your subject as "Television viewing" or "Viewing television," you can find either word in the "Rotated Section" and learn which form is used by *Psychological Abstracts* as a subject heading.

According to the *Thesaurus*, the relevant terms to use in the *Psychological Abstracts* subject indexes for this topic appear to be "Television," "Television viewing," "Mass media," and possibly "Violence," "Aggressive behavior," and "Aggressiveness." The last three are probably a little too broad and may lead to many irrelevant references. However, it might be necessary to look them up if the search of the first three headings is not fruitful.

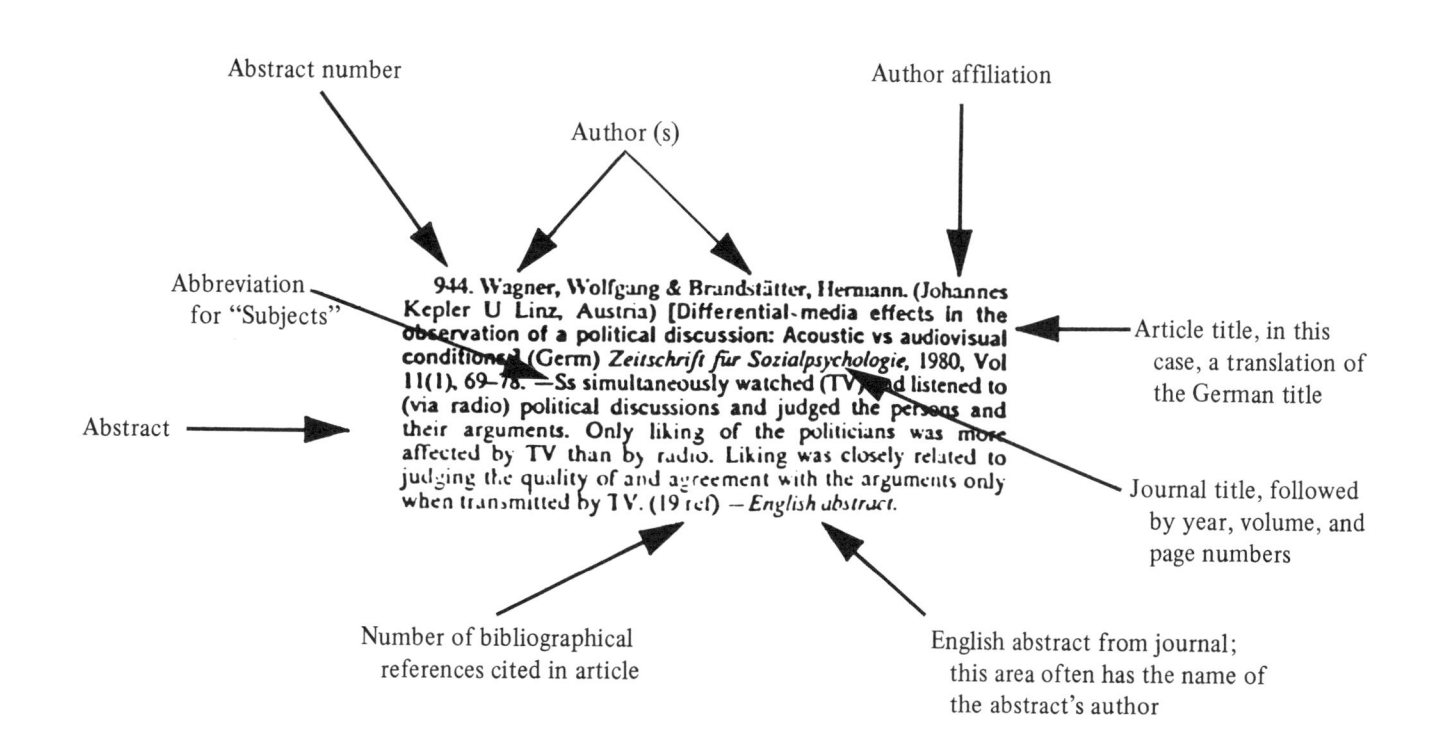

FIGURE 4.2. An abstract from Psychological Abstracts, vol. 66, no. 1 (July 1981)

TABLE OF CONTENTS

In the 16 major content classifications, abstracts that are relevant to a major category but not to any of the subsections are listed first and followed by abstracts that are relevant both to a major category and also to the subsection.

	abstract number	page number
GENERAL PSYCHOLOGY	1	1
Parapsychology	9	1
History & Philosophies & Theories	20	3
Research Methods & Apparatus & Computer Applications	35	4
PSYCHOMETRICS	131	11
Test Construction & Validation	145	13
Statistics & Mathematics	243	22
EXPERIMENTAL PSYCHOLOGY (HUMAN)	293	26
Perception & Motor Processes	312	28
Visual Perception	341	32
Auditory & Speech Perception	399	38
Cognitive Processes	410	40
Learning & Memory	446	44
Motivation & Emotion	508	51
Attention & Consciousness States	515	52
EXPERIMENTAL PSYCHOLOGY (ANIMAL)	520	53

FIGURE 4.3. Psychological Abstracts, vol. 63, no. 1. Table of Contents.

Accepted term — **Television** [67]
   B Audiovisual Communications Media
      Communications Media
Broader term — Mass Media
      Telecommunications Media
Narrower term — N Closed Circuit Television
      Educational Television
Related term — Television Advertising
   R Apparatus

— Year term was entered into *Thesaurus* use.

Television Advertising [73]
   B Advertising
      Audiovisual Communications Media
      Communications Media
      Mass Media
      Telecommunications Media
      Television

Television Viewing [73]
   B Recreation

Cross reference — **Temperament**
from form not used   **Use** Personality/

Temperature (Body)
   Use Body Temperature

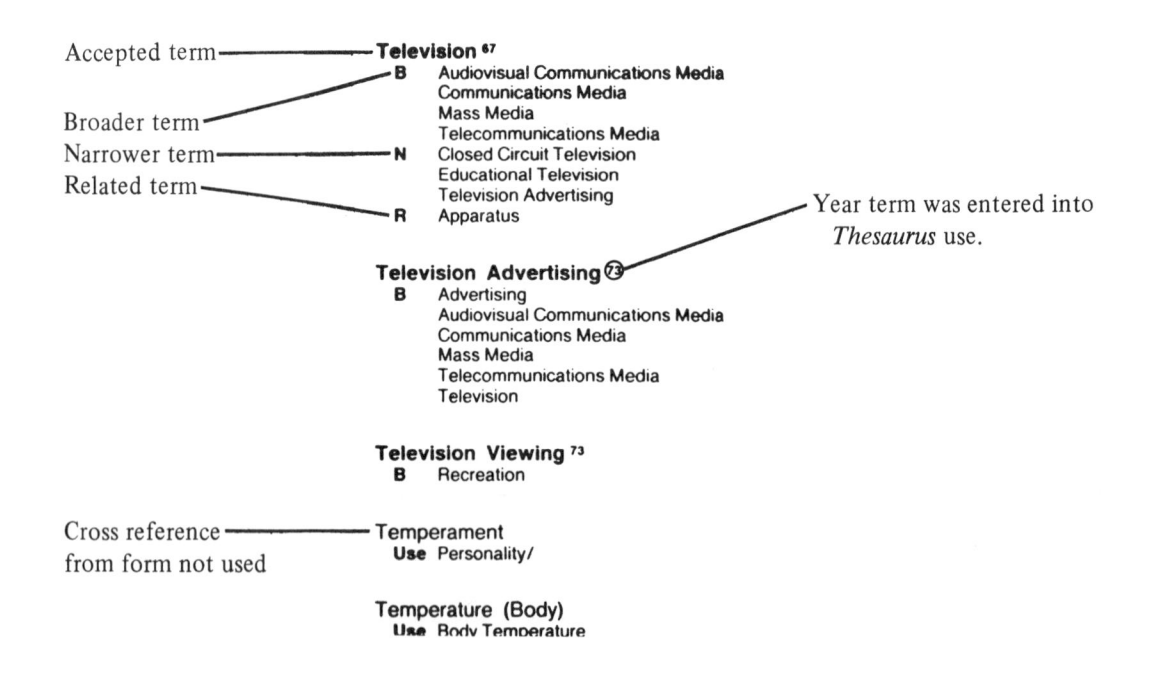

FIGURE 4.4. Thesaurus of Psychological Index Terms (1982). Relationship section.

```
                    Telepathy
                    Telephone Systems
                    Televised Instruction
                    Television
                    Television Advertising
                    Television Viewing
    Closed Circuit  Television
    Educational     Television
Guilford Zimmerman  Temperament Surv
                    Temperature Effects
                    Temperature Perception
              Body  Temperature
              Skin  Temperature
```

FIGURE 4.5. Thesaurus of Psychological Index Terms (1982). Rotated alphabetical terms section.

Psychological Abstracts Subject Index

Every six months a cumulative subject index to *Psychological Abstracts* is issued. Headings from the *Thesaurus* are listed; then under each heading is a list of the abstracts which have been assigned that subject heading. The list is more than just a group of abstract numbers, however; it consists of groups of descriptive phrases followed by an abstract number. For each article, the phrases give first the general subject, then a phrase qualifying it, a description of the population studied, and finally sometimes a phrase indicating the type of article, such as "literature review." FIGURE 4.6 shows a section of the cumulative subject index for January-June 1981. Many aspects of "Television viewing" are listed; to select useful articles, you need to look for key words and phrases that reflect your topic. In the example, the phrases "TV news" and "awareness of violence" make abstract number 7577 interesting. The phrase "5-8 year olds" warns of the limitations of this research in regard to the age group studied.

In using the cumulated indexes, be careful to look for the abstract in the right issue of *Psychological Abstracts*. The numbering of the abstracts begins anew every six months. There are many abstracts numbered 7577, but only one 7577 in the January-June 1981 issues (FIGURE 4.7). Generally, you should start your search with the latest six months cumulated index and work back through earlier cumulations until you start seeing material you had covered in review articles or encyclopedias.

Before the six months cumulative index appears, you still have a subject approach available; you can use the "Brief Subject Index" in the back of each monthly issue. This index lists thesaurus terms, but the terms are followed only by a list of abstract numbers, with no descriptive phrases (see FIGURE 4.8). You must look at each abstract to determine its relevance to your research.

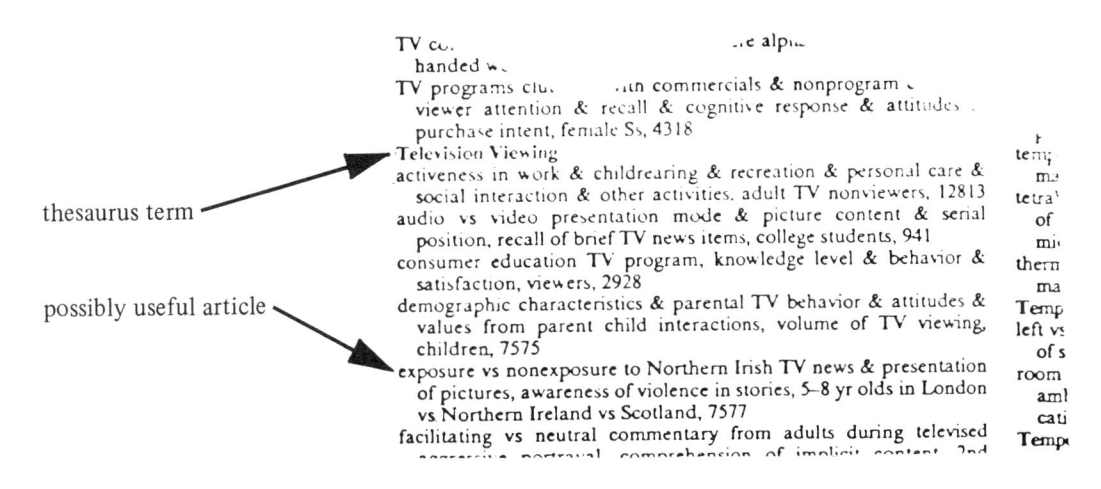

FIGURE 4.6. Psychological Abstracts, vol. 65, no. 6. Cumulated subject index.

7577. Cairns, Ed; Hunter, Dale & Herring, Linda. (New University of Ulster, Coleraine, Northern Ireland) **Young children's awareness of violence in Northern Ireland: The influence of Northern Irish television in Scotland and Northern Ireland.** *British Journal of Social & Clinical Psychology,* 1980(Feb), Vol 19(1), 3–6. —Describes 2 studies with 213 5–8 yr olds. In the preliminary study, 5–6 yr olds living in either a suburb of London or in a small town in Northern Ireland that has been virtually free from violence made up stories in response to pictures depicting such things as derelict houses or a train crash. More Northern Irish Ss mentioned bombs and explosions than did London Ss. A 2nd study investigated the possibility that this knowledge of explosions might be the result of exposure to coverage of such events on Northern Irish TV news. Ss from another relatively quiet part of Northern Ireland were compared with Ss from 2 separate areas of Scotland where TV reception is only possible from Northern Ireland and from a 3rd area in Scotland where Northern Ireland TV news cannot be received. Ss from those areas where Northern Irish TV news can be received again outnumbered those from the control area in terms of mentions of the words bomb or explosion. (5 ref) —*Journal abstract.*

FIGURE 4.7. Psychological Abstracts, vol. 65, April-June 1981.

---

tal Lo..., ...be, Visu...
7296, 7394, 743?
Telephone Hot Lines [See Hot Line Services]
Telephone Systems 8961, 8996
Television [See Also Educational Television, Television Advertising] 7077, 7078, 7741
Television Advertising 7576, 7904, 9028, 9030, 9036
→ Television Viewing 7575, 7577, 8793
Temperament [See Personality]
Temperature (Body) [See Body Temperature]
Temperature (Skin) [See Skin Temperature]
Temperature Effects [See Also Cold Effects

FIGURE 4.8. Psychological Abstracts, vol. 65, April 1981. Brief subject index.

Television —ed
"All in the Family," Dutch audience perceptions; ethnocentrism, intolerance, authoritarianism themes, differential effects prediction, selective exposure, perception retention: 78J3596
"All in the Family," racial humor perceptions, blacks vs whites; prejudice reduction vs increase, Deep South interviews, agreement, Archie Bunker, race relations: 78J3572
1972 report on television, social behavior, press coverage; content analysis, indefinite reporting, follow-ups scarcity, difficulty-enhancing factors: 78J3592
1976 New Hampshire primary, pre-election news coverage; televisions vs newspapers, candidate visibility, affinity variance: 78J2112
1976 televised presidential debate impact, voter political attitudes; Carter-Ford debate, issue awareness, campaign interest, candidate evaluation: 78J5155
adolescent television use, interpersonal factors; parents, siblings, friends, alone viewing contexts, communication patterns, social learning measures; US: 78J0548
antidrug commercials, impact assessment, hearers' negative attitudes, threats, boomerang effect explanation: 78J4731
Austria, Belgium, Tunisia, Yugoslavia, adolescents' media consumption; leisure activities, diversion, evasion functions, tastes diversity, economic, cultural, educational factors: 78J5511
Belgian televisi...   social education, specific pro...
  character...   ...cial functio...
Belg...
              ...ciations   ...s wishful
     ...ion impact: 78J1...
     ...n comedy, sexual humor; hostile vs nonhostile, sex discrimination, disparagement, prime family viewing time: 78J4445
television commercials, racism; mental illness assumption, negative portrayals, change possibilities: 78J4861
television content perceptions, community pluralism; realism, other-ideals, self-ideals, urban centers vs rural towns, identity reinforcement: 78J3593
television effects, political candidates, message impact; experimental study design, communicator evaluations, group vs individual judgments, B. Latané, social impact theory: 78J0651
television effects, reality vs fantasy roles; aggression increase, diminution mechanisms: 78J0552
television film, children's understanding; audience situation impact, empathic competency development: 78J1187
television impact, social behavior; saturation point, communication methods, German society, individualism trend: 78J3586
television interview shows, descriptive analysis; political office-holders, guests' voting records, party affiliation, visibility politics: 78J2080
television journalists, professionalism rating, performance relationship; McLeod-Hawley instrument, job duties, skillfulness, dissatisfaction levels: 78J2334
television news, attention, retention, comprehension; visualization impact, viewing frequency, recall, selectivity, issue-specific variations: 78J3578
television news, consciousness parameters; reflexivity suppression, socialization, normative considerations blockage, sociopolitical implications: 78S09684
television newspeople's power, US public's evaluations, party, ideology correlates; Republicans vs Democrats, Independents, age, education, political participation: 78J3728
television newswork, time factor; social organization, construction, hard news

FIGURE 4.9 Sociological Abstracts, vol. 26. Cumulated subject index.

Sociological Abstracts

Because the fields of psychology and sociology overlap significantly *Sociological Abstracts* (NY: Sociological Abstracts, 1952–) is also an appropriate index to search for your topic. *Sociological Abstracts* is published five times a year, and a cumulative index is published in the following year. Approximately 600 journals are scanned for indexing, and, in addition, papers presented at sociological meetings are indexed.

Sociological Abstracts is structured very much like *Psychological Abstracts*. The annual cumulative indexes add strings of descriptive terms to the entries just as the *Psychological Abstracts* cumulated indexes do. FIGURE 4.9 illustrates a section of the cumulated subject index for 1978. In the abstract number, the two digits preceding the alphabetic character refer to the year of *Sociological Abstracts* containing that particular abstract; this two digit prefix was discontinued in 1979. Abstract numbers with the letter "S" in them refer to papers presented at meetings. These abstracts are usually included near the end of each issue. In the same manner as *Psychological Abstracts*, there are brief subject indexes at the end of each issue which you can use before the annual cumulated index is published, but in *Sociological Abstracts* even the issue indexes have strings of descriptive terms.

Social Sciences Citation Index: Permuterm Index

In the next chapter, we will deal at some length with the *Social Sciences Citation Index (S.S.C.I.)* (Philadelphia: Institute for Scientific Information, 1973–), but for the present, we will discuss only the subject part of *S.S.C.I.*, the "Permuterm Index." The "Permuterm Index" does not use the thesaurus or standard terms approach of the other indexes; rather, it is a key word index that can be searched by every significant two-word combination derivable from the title (omitting articles, conjunctions, and other words of minor importance). Some enrichment words are added to titles which are not sufficiently descriptive. The two-word combinations are *not* limited to consecutive words, but use every pair regardless of their position in the title. *Social Sciences Citation Index* treats frequently used phrases such as GUINEA-PIG, NEW-YORK, and TELEVISION-NEWS as single indexing terms to facilitate matching these against other terms.

FIGURE 4.10 shows an example of a search under TELEVISION-NEWS as the first word, with the modifying word VIOLENCE. The author listed, Lichty, must be looked up in the "Source Index" portion of *S.S.C.I.* (FIGURE 4.11). The "Source Index" is an alphabetized list which gives full bibliographic citations for every item, including a list of the references cited in the article. More uses of the "Source Index" will be explained in the next chapter.

There are three reasons why you might want to use *Social Sciences Citation Index* to supplement a subject search of *Psychological Abstracts*: 1) it will usually index articles before they are indexed in *Psychological Abstracts*; 2) it indexes approximately 4,300 journals from the wide range of the social sciences, a wider scope than *Psychological Abstracts*; and 3) for some topics, the *S.S.C.I.* subject approach based on title words will give you better access to articles than the limited terminology allowed in *Psychological Abstracts* through the *Thesaurus of Psychological Index Terms*. However, the lack of a standardized terminology in *S.S.C.I.* can sometimes be a disadvantage. For instance, the combinations of TELEVISION plus VIOLENCE, TELEVISED plus VIOLENCE, and TELEVISION-NEWS plus VIOLENCE yield a total of 25 references — and only two references are duplicates (FIGURE 4.12). The lack of a standardized list means that you must be more careful to think of all possible useful terms. Try to think of synonyms, and even antonyms. For instance, research on the psychology of successful athletes might appear in the "Permuterm Index" under combinations including any of these terms: athletes, athletics, sports, competition, winning, losing, victory, defeat, success. Combining these terms would probably result in the same lack of duplicates that our television example showed in FIGURE 4.12. Generally, the more terms you try, the more citations you will find.

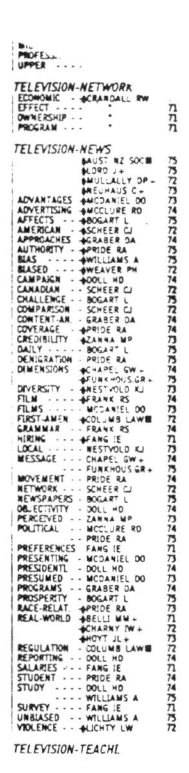

This shows that an entry appears for "Television News" and "Violence" by Lichty in the *1972* Source Index

FIGURE 4.10. Social Sciences Citation Index, 1971–75, vol. 15. Permuterm subject index.

Which Index to Use?

Your choice of index depends very much on the resources of your library and the nature of your topic. Most libraries have *Social Sciences Index*, and often its coverage of the most important psychology journals will be adequate for your research. Research that crosses the lines between psychology and the other social sciences is most profitably done using *Social Sciences Index, Sociological Abstracts*, and *Social Sciences Citation Index*. As your research becomes more advanced, or if you need an index to more journals specifically covering psychology, both *Psychological Abstracts* and *Social Sciences Citation Index* will become increasingly valuable to you. This is especially true if your library is large enough to have many of the journals indexed or if you can use interlibrary loan to obtain articles (see Chapter 8).

If your subject is closely related to psychiatry or neurology, or to specific subdivisions of psychology, there are alternative or supplemental indexes to use. For instance, in the area of psychiatry or neurology, or whenever a subject has a

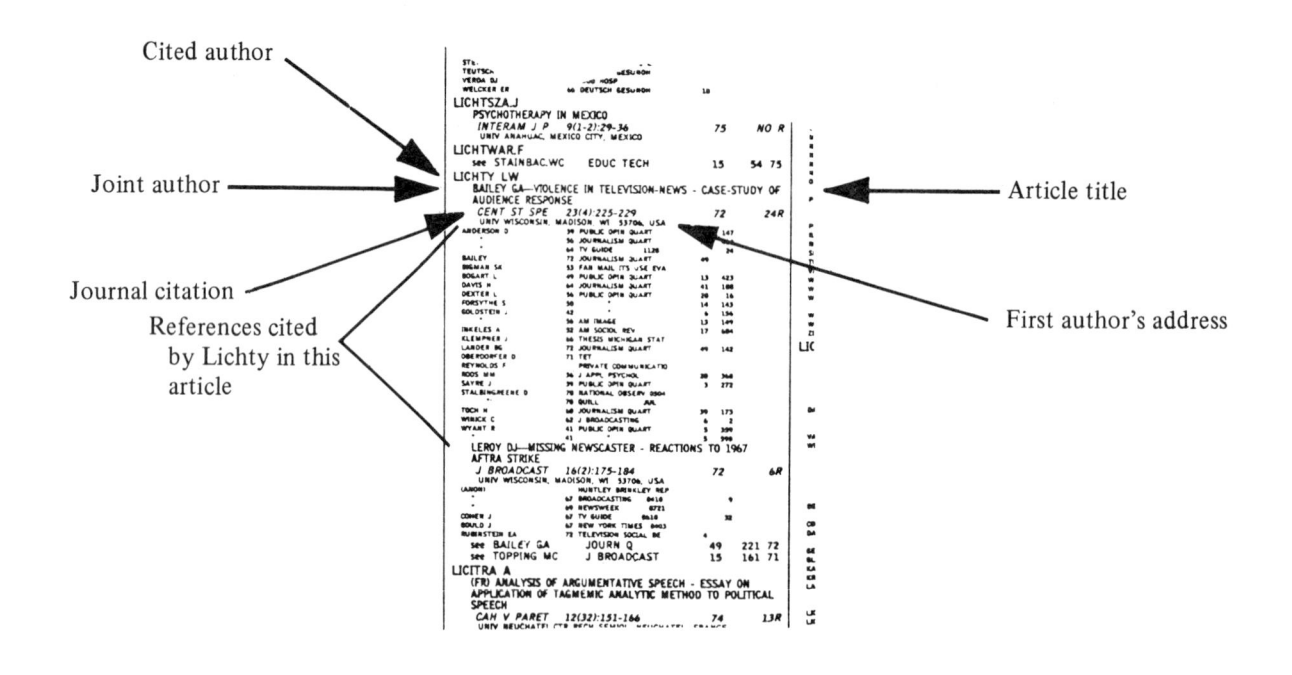

FIGURE 4.11. Social Sciences Citation Index, 1971–75, vol. 10. Source index.

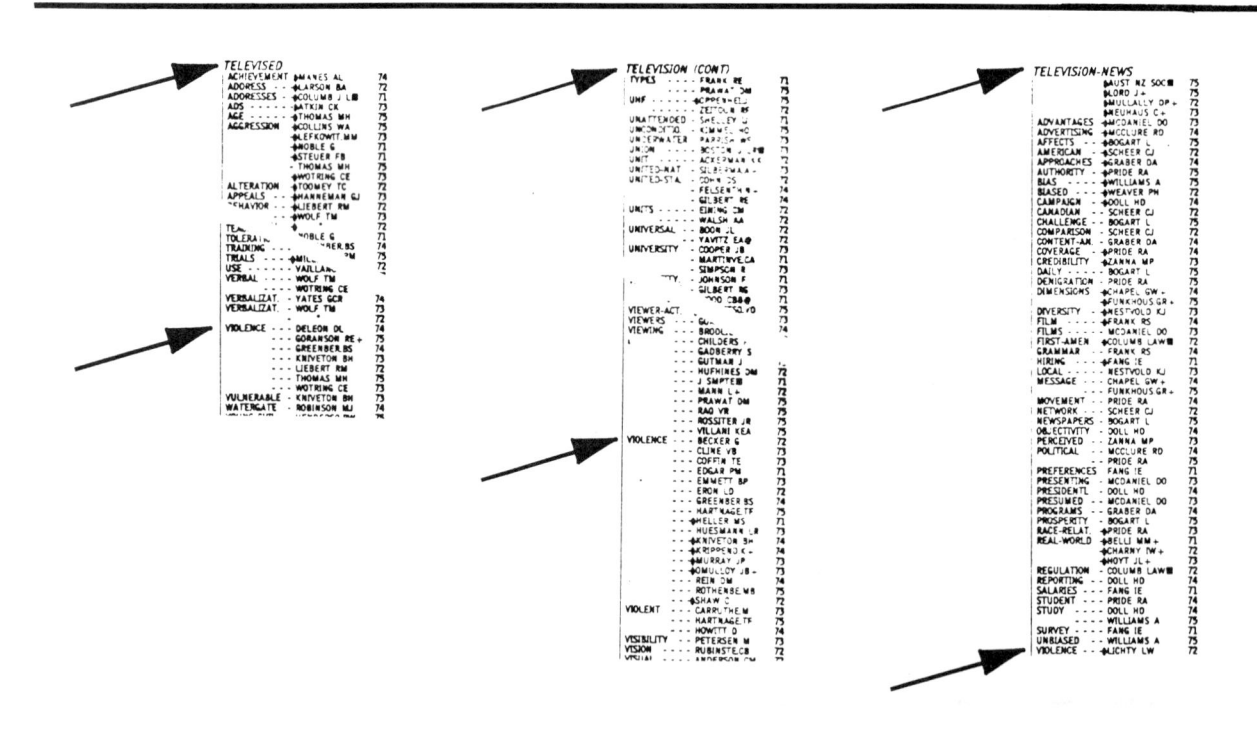

FIGURE 4.12. Social Sciences Citation Index, 1971–75. Permuterm index. A comparison of three search combinations.

medical dimension, *Index Medicus* (Washington, DC: National Library of Medicine, 1960–) should be used. For this reason, a chapter specifically on *Index Medicus* has been included in this guide as Appendix II. Several more of the most important specialized indexes are included in Appendix IV, a bibliography of reference sources useful for library work in specific areas of psychology. Your reference librarian can help you find others.

Computerized Literature Searching

In some cases, especially when you are doing research on a complex topic involving the relationship of several concepts, a computerized search of the literature may be the most effective procedure. For more than ten years now, most major publishers of periodical indexes and abstracting services have used computer technology to speed up and improve their operations. As a result, these indexing and abstracting services are available on computer tapes and can be searched by computer as an alternative to manually searching the printed volumes. Several commercial, government, and research organizations now maintain large data bases of bibliographic information, and more and more libraries are providing their patrons with access to these data bases. If your library has a computer searching service, you might want to investigate the possibility of using it in your research.

The most obvious advantage of computerized literature searching is speed. In less than ten minutes, a computer can search ten years of an index for references that would take hours to search manually, and then provide a printed bibliography of these references, with abstracts if they exist. Another advantage of most computer searches is enhanced subject access to the documents indexed. For example, in the printed volumes of *Psychological Abstracts* you are restricted to using the subject headings listed in the *Thesaurus of Psychological Index Terms*. The computerized version of *Psychological Abstracts* allows you to include title words and abstract words, *Thesaurus* terms, and the strings of descriptive phrases assigned for use in the cumulated subject indexes. Moreover, computer searching allows you to combine the concepts you are searching in order to retrieve only those documents likely to be most relevant to your topic. The words "television," "violence," and "news" can be typed in at the computer terminal, and the computer will retrieve only those references which include all three terms. The information in a computerized index is usually updated on the same schedule as the corresponding paper supplement; however, the paper copy requires time for printing, binding, and shipping, while the computerized updated index is immediately available.

How to Get a Computer Search Done

To get a computer search done, you must go to your library's computer searching service and have a librarian perform the search for you. In advance, you will need to spend some time preparing a clear, concise statement of your topic. You will also need to list those words and phrases that are likely to appear in the title, abstracts, subject headings, and descriptive phrases of the documents which would be of interest to you.

Together with the librarian, you will select and group these words and phrases in such a manner as to retrieve the most relevant references from the data bases you choose to search. Because the librarian will actually perform the search for you, you need not be familiar with the computer commands that are used in the search.

FIGURE 4.13 shows a sample computer search of the *Psychological Abstracts* data base from 1967 to June 1980 on the subject of the depiction of violence in television or mass media news reports. This particular search was done on the Bibliographic Retrieval Services (BRS) version of the *Psychological Abstracts* data base. (BRS is just one of the organizations which maintains computer files of bibliographical information. Two other such organizations are Dialog Information Services and Systems Development Corporation.) In this search, three search statements were used to define the three concepts in which you are interested: violence, television, and news. Truncation is used in order to

```
BRS - SEARCH MODE - ENTER QUERY
    1_:     VIOLEN$ OR AGGRESS$
    RESULT     8020

    2_:     MASS ADJ MEDIA OR TELEVIS$ OR TV
    RESULT     1937

    3_:     NEWS$
    RESULT     871

    4_:     1 AND 2 AND 3
    RESULT     11
```

FIGURE 4.13. Sample search of Psychological Abstracts using Bibliographic Retrieval Services.

save time; thus, in the first search statement the term "VIOLEN$" is used instead of typing in "violent," "violently," "violence." In other words, "VIOLEN$" will pick up any word that begins with the string of characters "violen." The result of the first search statement is 8020. This means that the computer found eight thousand and twenty references (hits) which had at least one of the words in the first search statement in their titles, abstracts, subject headings, or descriptive strings. Similarly, the second search statement resulted in 1837 hits and the third in 871 hits. In the next statement, we ask for the intersection of these three groups of references and select those which appear in all three groups. These will be references which have at least one term from each of the three groups of terms in their titles, abstracts, subject headings, or descriptive strings. The result of this operation is 11 hits; that is, 11 references in the *Psychological Abstracts* data base which have at least one word from each of the three concepts we have defined. These 11 references are most likely to be relevant to your topic.

The information in the references can be printed as concisely or fully as you want, with options ranging from just the *Psychological Abstracts* volume and abstract number, to the complete record including the abstract. FIGURE 4.14 shows a complete record for one of the items retrieved from this search. The information is similar to what you would find in the printed abstract, although the format is somewhat different and some additional information is provided. For example, the computer will print out the subject headings assigned to the article (in the "MJ" section or field) and the string of descriptive phrases (in the "ID" field). Typically, then, what you get back from a computer search is a tailor-made bibliography (with or without abstracts) on the subject of your choice. (NOTE: Over 100 bibliographical data bases can be searched at present, including *Sociological Abstracts* and the *Social Sciences Citation Index*.)

When Should You Have a Computer Search Done?

Although there are many advantages to having a computer search done, there are some disadvantages as well. First of all, most libraries will pass on part or all of the costs of computer searching to the search requester. Another disadvantage is that most of the computerized data bases do not go back very far; usually they start in the early or mid 1970s. Consequently, if you are working on a topic which requires you to do a search of the literature before 1970, you would have to supplement your computer search with a manual search, although the references in the articles you get from a computer search should give you a good selection of the earlier literature. However, if you are working on an important research paper and have a complex topic which involves the relationship of several different concepts, a computer search is worth considering, especially if you are pressed for time.

```
AN  00645 60-1.
AU  FRAZIER-SHERVERT-H.
IN  MCLEAN HOSP, BELMONT, MA.
TI  MASS MEDIA AND PSYCHIATRIC DISTURBANCE.
SO  PSYCHIATRIC JOURNAL OF THE UNIVERSITY OF OTTAWA.   1976 DEC VOL 1(4)
    171-172.
LG  EN.
YR  76
CC  2700 2800.
PT  10.
MJ  TELEVISION-VIEWING.  VIOLENCE.  AGGRESSIVE-BEHAVIOR.  CHILDREN.
    LITERATURE-REVIEW.
AB  EXAMINES THE RELATIONSHIP BETWEEN TV AND VIOLENCE, AS REPORTED BY THE
    SURGEON GENERAL'S SCIENTIFIC ADVISORY COMMITTEE ON TELEVISION AND SOCIAL
    BEHAVIOR (1972) AND BY OTHER STUDIES.  IT IS SUGGESTED THAT THE IMPACT
    OF NEWS COVERAGE ON CHILDREN IS MORE SHATTERING AND BEWILDERING THAN
    THEIR SO-CALLED "FORBIDDEN PROGRAMS," BECAUSE NEWS PROGRAMS (A) INVOLVE
    REAL PEOPLE AND VIOLENCE, (B) OFTEN TAKE PLACE IN SETTINGS SIMILAR TO THE
    VIEWER'S OWN SETTING, AND (C) DO NOT SHOW THE AGGRESSOR BEING PUNISHED
    (AS GENERALLY IS DONE IN SERIES PROGRAMS).  THE AUTHOR CITES E. FROMM'S
    (1968) 3 CLASSES OF AGGRESSIVENESS AND OBSERVES THAT SUCH TYPES ARE NOT
    MUTUALLY EXCLUSIVE BUT OFTEN OCCUR IN COMBINATIONS.  (17 REF).
ID  TV NEWS VS OTHER PROGRAMS, INSTIGATION OF VIOLENCE & AGGRESSIVE BEHAVIOR,
    CHILDREN, LITERATURE REVIEW.
```

FIGURE 4.14. Sample reference with abstract from search of Psychological Abstracts using Bibliographic Retrieval Services.

"(Gasp...) Indexes, INDEXES...

Summary

1. The most important subject indexes to original research published in psychology periodicals are *Social Sciences Index, Psychological Abstracts, Sociological Abstracts,* and the "Permuterm Index" to *Social Sciences Citation Index.*

2. Since *Social Sciences Index* is held by most libraries and indexes the most important and widely held periodicals in psychology and related fields, it is often a good place to start your literature search.

3. If *Social Sciences Index* is not available or if it doesn't seem to cover your topic well, you should use *Psychological Abstracts, Sociological Abstracts,* or *Social Sciences Citation Index. Psychological Abstracts* and *Social Sciences Citation Index* both cover many more psychology periodicals than the other two indexes.

4. *Psychological Abstracts* coverage is most specifically psychology; the other indexes have interdisciplinary aspects. For medical topics, see *Index Medicus* (Appendix II), and for other specialized disciplines see Appendix IV and your reference librarian.

5. The approaches to subject searching differ in the four indexes: *Social Sciences Index* and *Sociological Abstracts* use a standardized vocabulary with cross references; *Psychological Abstracts* uses a list of terms called the *Thesaurus of Psychological Index Terms; Social Sciences Citation Index* rotates words from article titles in its "Permuterm Index."

6. When your time is short or your topic is complex, a computerized literature search might be worth its cost to you.

5 The Author Approach: *Social Sciences Citation Index*

> "Choose an author as you choose a friend."
> — Wentworth Dillon, Essay on Translated Verse

After using encyclopedias, review journals and subject indexes, you may feel you have sufficient book and periodical resources to write your research paper. However, when you are aware of certain authors who have written key books or articles on your topic, it is a good idea to try to find out what else these authors have written. In many cases, their more recent works will update or revise their earlier research. In addition, it would be interesting to discover what other researchers have written in reaction to the work of these authors.

Finding other articles by an author can be done fairly easily with all of the indexes which we have previously discussed. *Social Sciences Index* lists authors alphabetically within its subject listings, and *Psychological Abstracts* and *Sociological Abstracts* have author indexes in both the individual issues and the cumulations. An author discovered through the subject approach may be worth researching in these author indexes. For example, in working with *Psychological Abstracts* in Chapter 4 we turned up abstract 7577 by Ed Cairns. In the *Psychological Abstracts* author index, two other numbers are listed by his name (see FIGURE 5.1). *Social Sciences Citation Index* goes a step beyond the other indexes in that it also lets you know which researchers have cited a particular author's work in their own research.

How Social Sciences Citation Index Is Constructed

The *Social Sciences Citation Index (S.S.C.I.)* coverage begins with 1966. It currently indexes the articles, editorials, letters, news items and which appear in over 4,300 periodicals in the social sciences, and also indexes some books. Some of the periodicals are only selectively indexed, but for each article chosen for indexing, the procedure is the same: the *S.S.C.I.* staff takes all citations from the article's bibliography and rearranges them, making the citations the major element and listing under each citation the author who cited it. For example, FIGURE 5.2 shows parts of a journal article: the author and title of the article, the name of the journal in which it appeared, the volume and page of the journal, and part of the bibliography of the article. Illustrated at the bottom of FIGURE 5.2 is the standardized format into which all this information is converted by the *S.S.C.I.* staff. Through computer manipulation, the hundreds of thousands of index entries are assembled into one master list, alphabetized by *cited* author — a citation index (FIGURE 5.3).

How to Use the "Citation Index"

By looking up some of the key books or articles discovered through your initial research, you can tell who has cited them and effectively update the information gathered thus far. For example, Howitt's book on violence and the mass media, published in 1975, can be traced from that year to the present. FIGURE 5.3 shows you what the 1979 "Citation Index" of *S.S.C.I.* lists under Howitt's name. Notice that Howitt has written another book and several articles which were cited by various authors in 1979. However, you are only interested in his 1975 book about violence and the mass media. As FIGURE 5.3 illustrates, the "Citation Index" shows that five authors have cited Howitt's book during 1979. You can expect, therefore, that the works of these authors have something to do with the subject of Howitt's book. However, to get some clue as to whether these works are indeed relevant, you need to go on to the "Source Index."

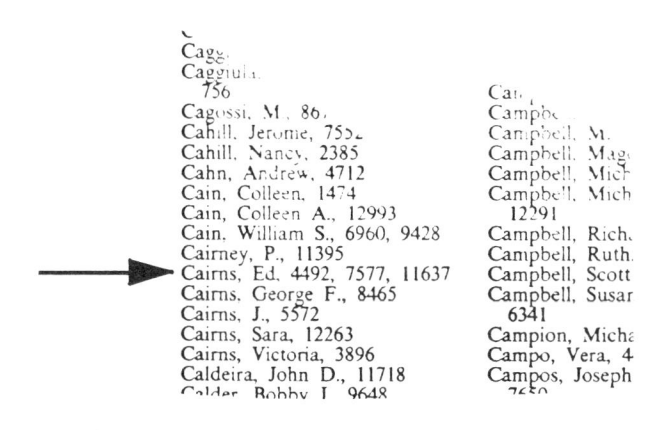

FIGURE 5.1. Psychological Abstracts, vol. 65, no. 6, pt. 2. Cumulative author index.

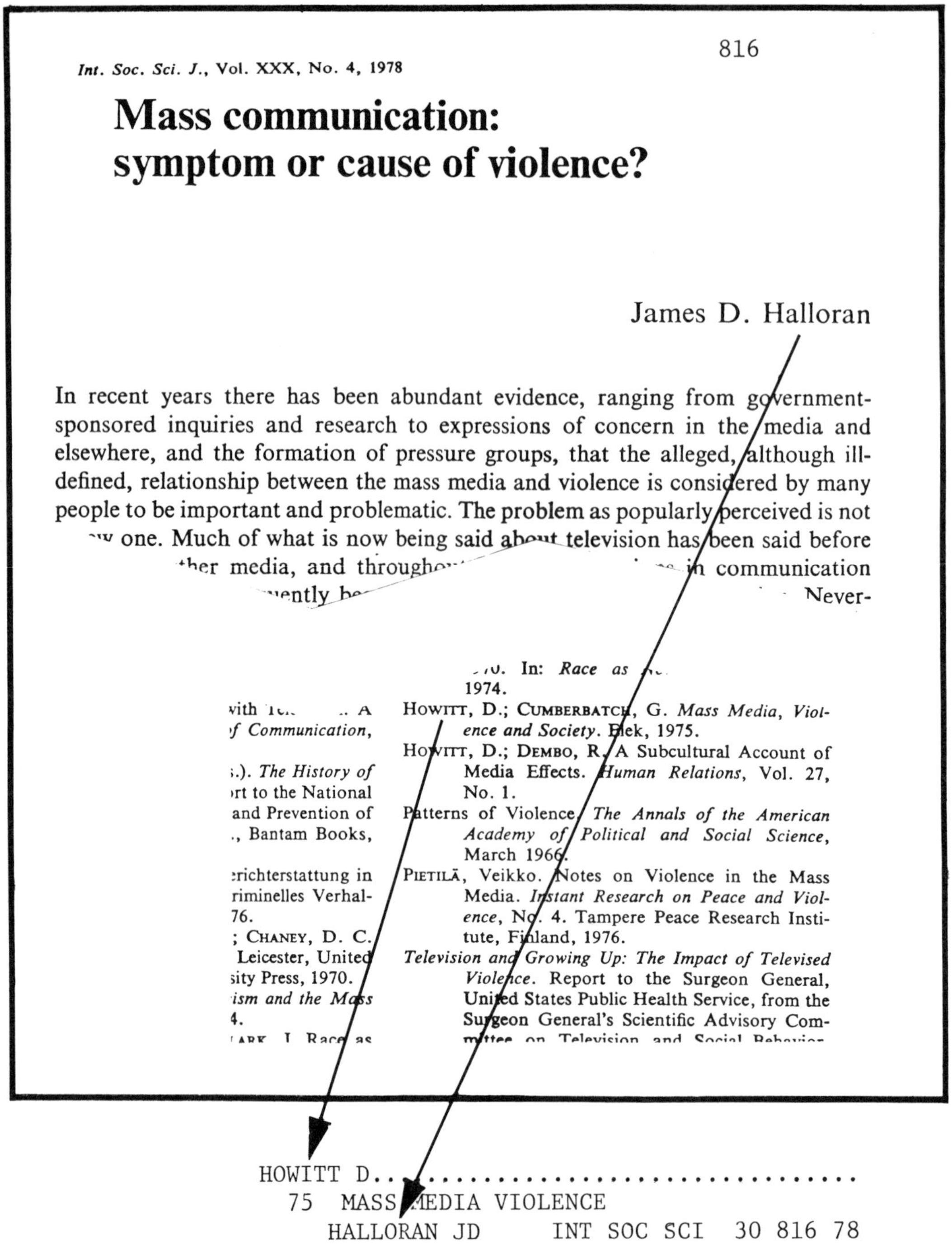
816

Int. Soc. Sci. J., Vol. XXX, No. 4, 1978

Mass communication: symptom or cause of violence?

James D. Halloran

In recent years there has been abundant evidence, ranging from government-sponsored inquiries and research to expressions of concern in the media and elsewhere, and the formation of pressure groups, that the alleged, although ill-defined, relationship between the mass media and violence is considered by many people to be important and problematic. The problem as popularly perceived is not ...w one. Much of what is now being said about television has been said before ...ther media, and through... ...n communication ...ently ... Never-

...vith ... A ...f *Communication*, ...). *The History of* ...rt to the National and Prevention of ., Bantam Books, ...richterstattung in ...riminelles Verhal- ...76. ; CHANEY, D. C. Leicester, United ...sity Press, 1970. ...*ism and the Mass* ...4. ...ARK, J. Race as

...70. In: *Race as* ... 1974.

HOWITT, D.; CUMBERBATCH, G. *Mass Media, Violence and Society*. Elek, 1975.

HOWITT, D.; DEMBO, R. A Subcultural Account of Media Effects. *Human Relations*, Vol. 27, No. 1.

Patterns of Violence. *The Annals of the American Academy of Political and Social Science*, March 1966.

PIETILÄ, Veikko. Notes on Violence in the Mass Media. *Instant Research on Peace and Violence*, No. 4. Tampere Peace Research Institute, Finland, 1976.

Television and Growing Up: The Impact of Televised Violence. Report to the Surgeon General, United States Public Health Service, from the Surgeon General's Scientific Advisory Committee on Television and Social Behavior

FIGURE 5.2. How a citation is indexed in Social Science Citation Index.

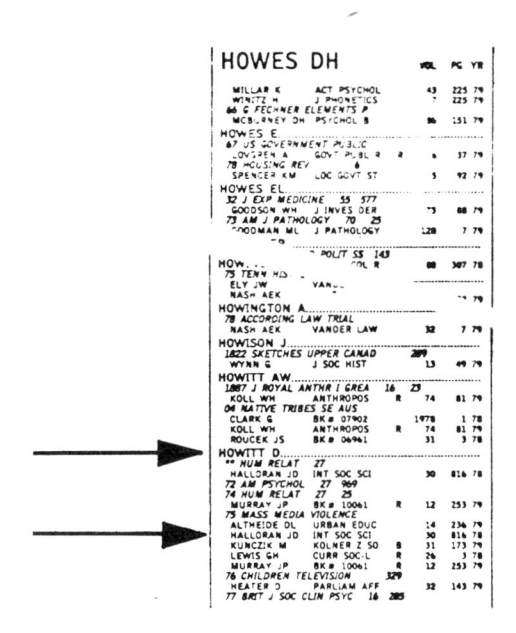

FIGURE 5.3. Social Sciences Citation Index, 1979, vol. 1, Citation index.

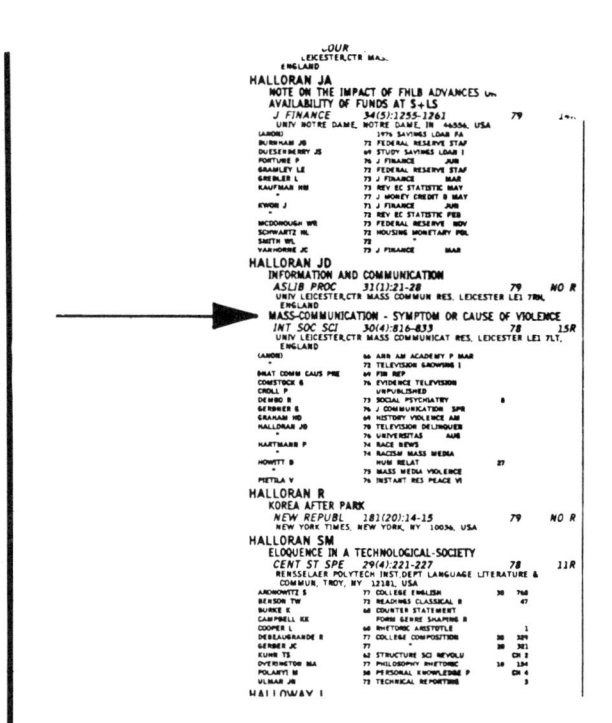

FIGURE 5.4. Social Sciences Citation Index, 1979, vol. 3, Source index.

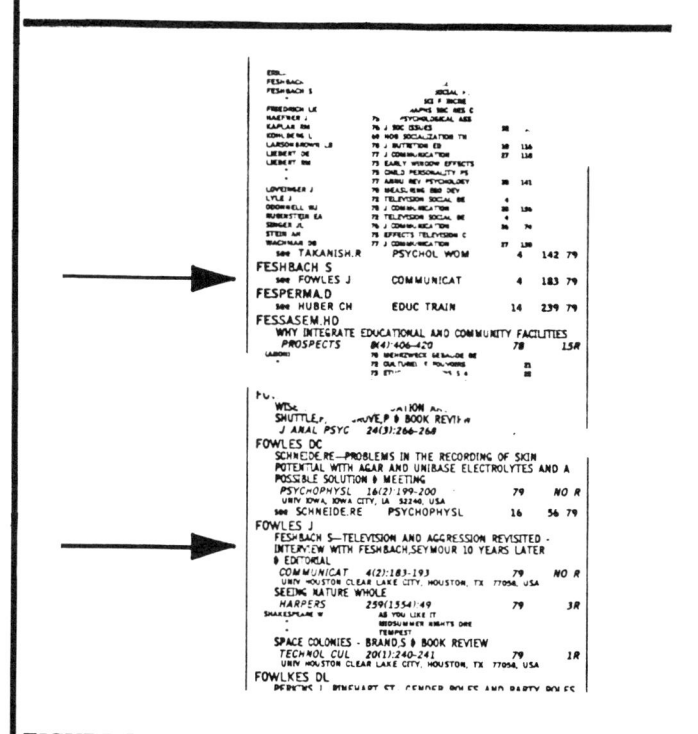

FIGURE 5.5. Social Sciences Citation Index, 1979, vol. 3, "Source index."

How to Use the "Source Index"

As we mentioned briefly in Chapter 4, the "Source Index" is an author list which gives the full bibliographic citation for all the books and articles which appear in the "Citation Index" or "Permuterm Subject Index." You can use the "Source Index" to look up any of the five authors who cited Howitt's book. For example, FIGURE 5.4 shows the entries in the 1979 "Source Index" for J.D. Halloran. The second entry by Halloran is the one which the "Citation Index" lists as citing Howitt's book. Because you now have the title of Halloran's article, "Mass-communication — Symptom or Cause of Violence," you can more readily determine its relevance to your subject. In addition, all the references in Halloran's article are listed, providing further potential references for your research. Finally, because all of Halloran's articles published in 1979 (in journals indexed by *S.S.C.I.*) are listed, you can also get some idea of his research interests. (Note: Since only initials are used, it is possible that two or more authors with the same last name and initials may be listed together.)

More than just research articles are indexed by *S.S.C.I.* Each periodical article may list various kinds of sources in its bibliography: books, articles, interviews, etc. These cited sources also appear in *S.S.C.I.* For example, the *International Encyclopedia of Psychiatry, Psychology, Psychoanalysis, and Neurology* lists S. Feshbach's book *Television and Aggression* (1971) as a key source in this field. It is a good idea to search Feshbach in the *S.S.C.I.* to see if he has written anything else on the subject. FIGURE 5.5 (top) shows you the 1979 *S.S.C.I.* "Source Index" which refers you from Feshbach to Fowles. FIGURE 5.5 (bottom) shows that the Fowles item is actually an interview with Feshbach about his book and therefore should provide a useful update to the book.

Tips on the Use of Social Sciences Citation Index

You may want to search each of your books or articles through all years of the citation index since each was published. Howitt's book could be searched in the "Citation Index" for the years 1975 up through the latest issue of *S.S.C.I. Social Sciences Citation Index* is published three times a year, the first two issues covering January-April and May-August and the third cumulating the others and completing the indexing to December of that year. Five-year cumulative issues of *S.S.C.I.* have also been published to make searching faster and easier.

As you search through the "Citation Index," beginning with the year your original article was published, you will discover more articles on your topic. You should incorporate them into your list and search them in the "Citation Index," too. This process permits you to build a larger, more complete bibliography of the most current literature on your topic.

In your work with *Social Sciences Citation Index* you may eventually come to the point where certain names continue to reappear and a select group of articles always refers to some or all of the articles you have on your list. When this happens, you have identified the essential core of the literature on your topic, as defined by workers in the field. Do not be too concerned if your research does not result in such a closely related set of articles, however; it is more frequently a reflection of the field of study than of the effectiveness of your search. *S.S.C.I.* contains a wealth of material, and in some cases you may feel you could add articles infinitely. You will need to keep comparing the citations to the central topic of your research paper and try to select only those citations which clearly focus on your topic. When you finish searching *S.S.C.I.*, you are ready to study the collection of new articles you have identified. You will want to take notes as you read them and relate their findings to those of the earlier articles. In studying the new articles you may discover still more new authors and papers you had not known about before. If you find them helpful, check them through the "Citation Index" as well.

Other Author Approaches

To conclude this chapter, it should be pointed out that if in your search several authors stand out as the preeminent authors on your topic you should do a thorough author search. First use the "Source Index" of *S.S.C.I.*; then use the author indexes of the other indexing tools we explained in Chapter 4 and listed in Appendix IV. *S.S.C.I.* is an extremely useful research tool, but not all libraries have it. If your library does not have *Social Sciences Citation Index*, you might want to consider going to visit another library. If you decide to do this, first read Chapter 8 "Using Other Libraries." Also, *Science Citation Index* (Philadelphia: Institute for Scientific Information, 1961–) is a very similar work which may be a useful alternative for research in psychiatry, neurology, and animal behavior.

Summary

1. There are two approaches to searching the periodical literature: the subject approach (Chapter 4) and the author approach (Chapter 5).

2. The primary tool for the author approach is the *Social Sciences Citation Index*.

3. To use *S.S.C.I.*, consult the "Citation Index" under the names of the authors whom you have on your list of relevant books and articles generated in Chapters 1–4. This will tell you who has cited these books and articles.

4. Then use the "Source Index" to determine the titles of the citing articles and thus help sort out the useful articles.

5. Each article on your list should be searched for all years since it was published up to the present.

6. When certain authors appear to dominate a field of study, a search for further articles by them would be appropriate. Use the "Source Index" of *S.S.C.I.* and the author indexes of such indexing tools as *Psychological Abstracts*.

6 The Last Six Months: Current Contents

> "Everything changes."
> — Marcus Aurelius,
> *Meditations*

In some fields of psychology, developments are occurring so rapidly that our understanding of particular phenomena may change in just a few months with the publication of significant new research findings. It is therefore necessary to get very recent material in order to understand the currently accepted theories or at least to understand the contradictory lines of evidence. As a student, you should also be aware that professors tend to have greater respect for papers which cite very recent work. You might even educate the professor by using sources of which he or she is not aware.

Unfortunately, even if you check all of the latest issues of the indexes mentioned in Chapters 4 and 5, you may be missing the most current material on your subject. The time lag between publication of an issue of a journal and publication of the index which analyzes it can be anywhere from eight weeks to a year or more. While indexes like *Psychological Abstracts* have made monumental efforts in recent years to reduce the gap, there remains a time period, generally about six months, between the literature covered in the most recent issue of an index and the time at which you are doing the search.

My psych professor said there's a periodical called "Worm Runner's Digest." Where are the latest issues?

How to Find Material Before It Is Indexed

The most obvious way to find material before it is indexed is simply to browse through the last few issues of those journals you have already found most useful. This has limitations, however; it is inconvenient to browse through dozens of issues of several different titles, and you may not have immediate access to all the important journals you want.

The convenient solution to the problem of gaining access to current periodicals which are not yet indexed is *Current Contents* (Philadelphia: Institute for Scientific Information, 1961–). It is organized and specifically designed to give rapid access to current literature, and does not serve as a permanent retrospective indexing tool. That is why *Current Contents* is referred to as a "current awareness service." *Current Contents* consists of seven different subject sections, such as "Social and Behavioral Sciences" and "Life Sci-

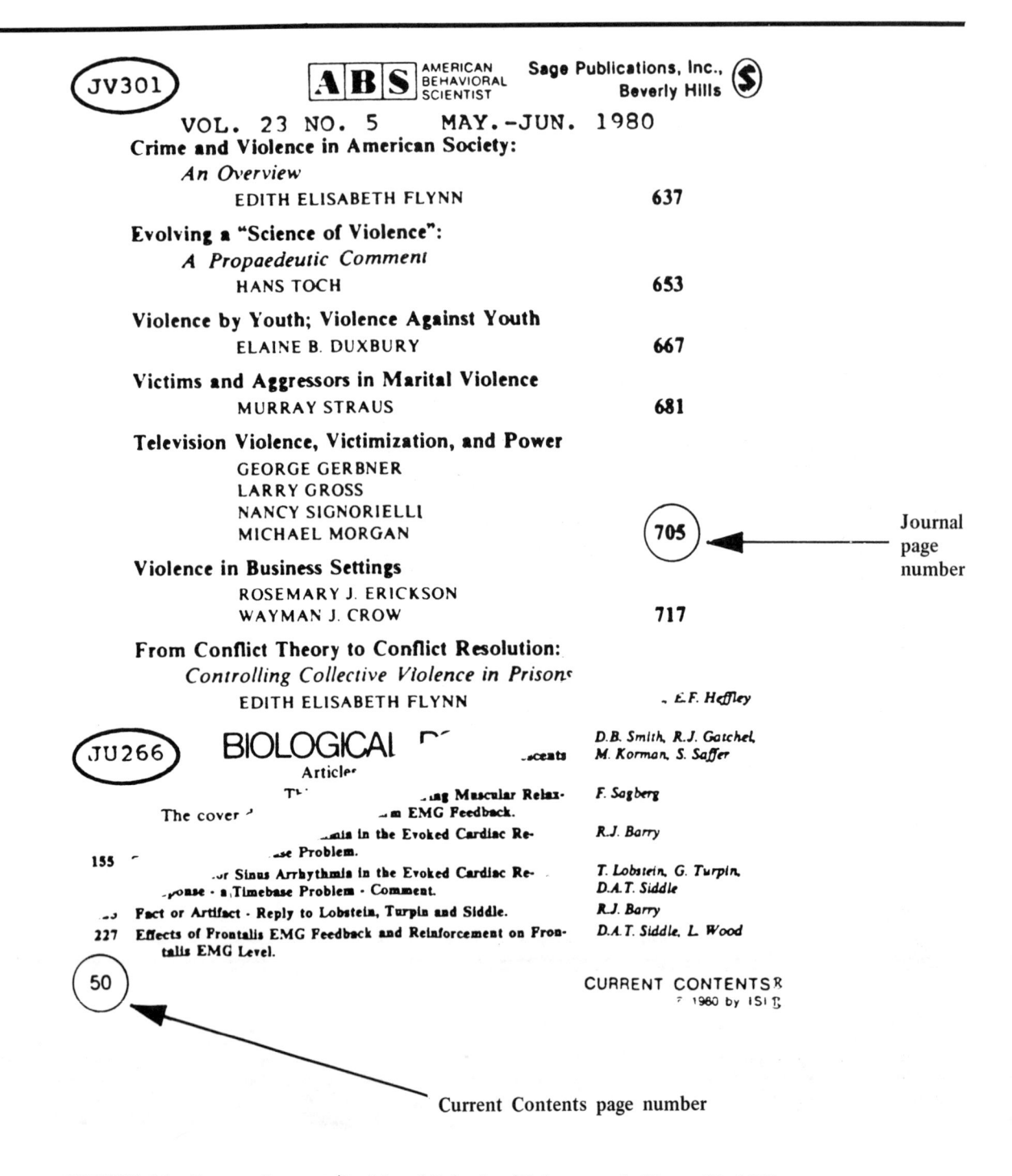

FIGURE 6.1. Current Contents/Social and Behavioral Sciences, vol. 12, no. 28, 1980.

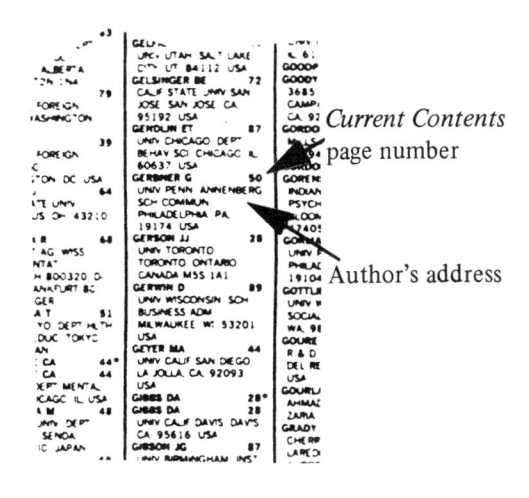

FIGURE 6.2. Current Contents/Social and Behavioral Sciences, vol 12, no. 28, 1980. Author index.

FIGURE 6.3. Current Contents/Social and Behavioral Sciences, vol. 12, no. 28, 1980. Subject index.

ences," each covering 700 to 1,100 journals, with some overlap. Each section is published weekly and includes copies of the Tables of contents of journals in the subject field (FIGURE 6.1) These tables of contents are generally less than six weeks old when they appear in *Current Contents*. Each issue of *Current Contents* contains an "Author Index" (FIGURE 6.2) and a "Subject Index" (FIGURE 6.3). *Current Contents* issues also have a list of journal titles and issue numbers for which contents are included.

Using Current Contents

The first problem you face is which subject section of *Current Contents* to use. This can be quickly solved by looking at the list of journals included, which is published at intervals in each section (FIGURE 6.4). The "Social and Behavioral Sciences" section lists journal titles which we discovered in our research on the relationship between television news violence and human aggressive behavior.

Once the appropriate section has been chosen there are three possible approaches. In each case, you should begin with the most recent issue of *Current Contents* and go backward until you begin relocating older articles you have already seen. The three approaches are as follows:

1. Search the "Author Index" (FIGURE 6.2) for names of workers in your area.

2. Search the "Subject Index" (FIGURE 6.3) for key terms. The first number in each entry refers to the page number in *Current Contents* and the second number refers to the page number in the journal's Table of Contents.

3. Use the list of journals covered in each issue to identify where Tables of Contents for journals important to your topic are located (FIGURE 6.4) and then browse through these Tables of Contents. Though this browsing approach is not too efficient for term paper research, it is sometimes used by scholars to keep up with on-going research in a particular field.

Summary

1. Rapid developments in psychology make it important to find the latest information.

2. Index coverage lags about eight weeks to a year behind the publication of the journals.

3. *Current Contents* provides access to recent issues of journals through the reprinting of their Tables of Contents. *Current Contents* has weekly journal title, author, and subject indexes, and occasional listings of journals covered. You will generally use the "Social and Behavioral Sciences" section for research in psychology.

4. *Current Contents* can be searched using names of important authors in a field, or by browsing Tables of Contents for key journals in the field, or by using the key word subject index.

VOLUME 14 NUMBER 1

January 4, 1982
Contents pages received thru
December 14, 1981

Not all journals covered by *Current Contents* are published weekly. Therefore, in any given issue your favorite journal may not be listed. However, it will be included as often as it is issued. For the latest Triannual Cumulative Index see issue #40, October 5, 1981.

In This Issue of CC®S&BS

Journal Coverage Changes	4
Current Comments®	5
ISI® Press Digest	14
Citation Classics	19
List of Serials & Publisher Guide	21
Current Book Contents®	39
Calling Attention To	50
Sociology/Anthropology/Linguistics	51
Social Issues & Philosophy	62
Psychology	68
Request-A-Print® Advertisement	R-1
Psychiatry	82
Public Health & Social Medicine	87
Rehabilitation & Special Education	91
Education	93
Library & Information Science	99
Geography, Planning & Development	102
Political Science & History	103
Law	112
Economics & Business	114
Management	120
Weekly Subject Index	126
Author Index & Address Directory	144
Publishers Address Directory	156

The publisher's name appears with the journal title of each contents page unless the name is contained within or is the same as the journal title. The address of each publisher is provided at the end of this issue. For Russian journals, contact a subscription agency.

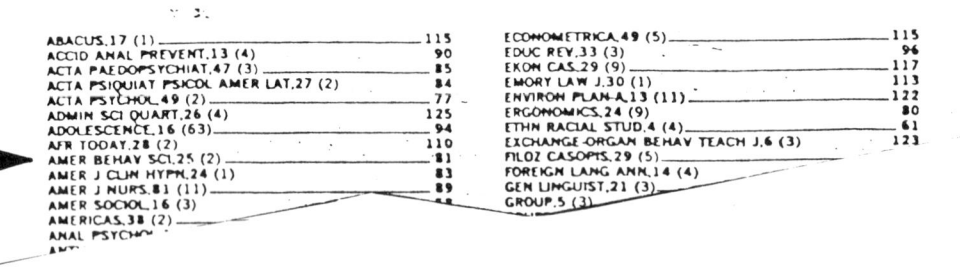

ABACUS,17 (1)	115	ECONOMETRICA,49 (5)	115
ACCID ANAL PREVENT,13 (4)	90	EDUC REV,33 (3)	96
ACTA PAEDOPSYCHIAT,47 (3)	85	EKON CAS,29 (9)	117
ACTA PSIQUIAT PSICOL AMER LAT,27 (2)	84	EMORY LAW J,30 (1)	113
ACTA PSYCHOL,49 (2)	77	ENVIRON PLAN-A,13 (11)	122
ADMIN SCI QUART,26 (4)	125	ERGONOMICS,24 (9)	80
ADOLESCENCE,16 (63)	94	ETHN RACIAL STUD,4 (4)	61
AFR TODAY,28 (2)	110	EXCHANGE-ORGAN BEHAV TEACH J,6 (3)	123
AMER BEHAV SCI,25 (2)	81	FILOZ CASOPIS,29 (5)	
AMER J CLIN HYPN,24 (1)	83	FOREIGN LANG ANN,14 (4)	
AMER J NURS,81 (11)	89	GEN LINGUIST,21 (3)	
AMER SOCIOL,16 (3)		GROUP,5 (3)	
AMERICAS,38 (2)			
ANAL PSYCH...			

FIGURE 6.4. Current Contents/Social and Behavioral Sciences, vol. 14, no. 1, 1982.

7 Using Guides to the Literature of Psychology

> "Knowledge is of two kinds: we know a subject ourselves, or we know where we can find information on it."
> — Samuel Johnson, quoted in Boswell's *Life of Johnson*

Why Use a Guide?

This book is a *selective* guide to the basic reference sources in psychology and therefore may not answer all your questions. Appendix IV of this book lists some other reference materials related to specific undergraduate courses in psychology, but you may need a more comprehensive guide in order to find specialized reference sources useful for your topic. Guides, which may select "best books" in the literature of a subject or serve as comprehensive lists of reference sources, can lead to materials in your library and can also point to the existence of materials not in your library collection. Reference librarians rely heavily on these guides and lists, and if finding enough materials is a problem, use of the guides may be the solution. The main difficulty with comprehensive guides is in selecting the few important sources from the many that are cited. Unfortunately, another major problem in psychology is that the two standard guides, listed below, were published back in 1971 and 1973. Even so, they are the best available and still useful. Be sure to consult your reference librarian for the newest editions or more current guides.

How to Use a Guide in Psychology

One useful comprehensive guide to reference sources in psychology is J.E. Bell's *A Guide to Library Research in Psychology* (Dubuque, Iowa: Wm. C. Brown, 1971). However, its most valuable feature is not the reference sources but the section on literature sources in major subject areas of interest to psychology students, including abnormal, social, experimental, educational, industrial, and applied psychology, and some fields related to psychology. For each field there are extensive lists of journal titles and basic texts. Although there is no index, the book has a good, detailed table of contents. FIGURE 7.1 shows how to use the Table of Contents to find basic readings in industrial psychology.

Another useful guide to the literature of psychology is C.M. White's *Sources of Information in the Social Sciences: A Guide to the Literature*, 2d ed. (Chicago: American Library Association, 1973) which has information on all of the social sciences, with a major section devoted to psychology. In the psychology section, the sources are arranged by type (such as encyclopedias, reviews, tests) and by major subject areas, and each source listed includes a detailed description. The subject, author, and title indexes make this book particularly useful in helping you find works in other social science areas which may be related to your topic (FIGURE 7.2).

How to Use General Reference Sources

The most comprehensive bibliographies of reference sources in English are A.J. Walford, *Guide to Reference Material*, 4th ed. (London: The Library Association, (1980--) and Eugene P. Sheehy, *Guide to Reference Books*, 9th ed. (Chicago: American Library Association, 1976), *Supplement*, 1980. Volume 2 of Walford has a section on psychology, and Sheehy has six pages. These two guides provide less depth of coverage in the field of psychology than White and Bell, but can be used if the others are not available in your library. They are also excellent in helping you find books in related fields. FIGURE 7.3 shows how the 1980 *Supplement* to Sheehy's work can be used to update the list of sources in Bell. (Note: The last item shown in FIGURE 7.3 is the American Psychological Association *Publication Manual*, which is also listed in Appendix IV with other "Handbooks for Writing Psychology Papers." The *Publication Manual* demonstrates the correct way to prepare psychology research reports for publication in periodicals; this is often the style preferred by psychology professors for term papers, as well.)

Summary

1. Guides to the literature of psychology may help you locate more specialized materials.

2. Comprehensive guides to the literature of the social sciences or to reference books in general may help you locate materials in related fields.

3. See also Appendix IV.

4. Your reference librarian can help you find revised editions or new guides to areas of research.

contents   ix

	Page
Bibliographies of Bibliographies	90
Miscellaneous	90
Lists of Published Books	90
Current Books	90
Older Books	91
Paperback Books	92
Psychology Paperback Books	92
Lists of Periodicals	92
All Periodicals	92
Psychology Periodicals	92
Education Periodicals	93
Journals	93
Abnormal Psychology	93
Developmental Psychology	94
Educational Psychology	94
Experimental Psychology	95
Personality and Social Psychology	96
Other Psychological Journals	96
Nonpsychological Periodicals	97
U.S. Government Psychological Periodicals	97
Lists of Textbooks and Books of Readings	98
Introductory Textbooks	98
Readings on Introductory Psychology	102
Introductions to Psychological Research	105
Developmental Psychology	106
Readings on Developmental Psychology	112
Exceptional Children	115
Readings on Exceptional Children	117
Books Which Describe and Discuss Piaget's Work	118
Social Psychology	119
Readings on Social Psychology	123
Industrial and Organizational Psychology	126
Readings on Industrial and Organizational Psychology	127
Applied Psychology	128

   .. *Work and* ... ⌐к: Wiley, 1964.

⌐, William. *Organizational* ⌐ ⌐ulor: *theory and application.* Homewood, Ill.: Dorsey, 1969.

Readings on Industrial and Organizational Psychology

Bennis, Warren et al. (Eds.) *The planning of change.* (2nd ed.) New York: Holt, Rinehart & Winston, 1969.

Cummings, Larry (Ed.) *Readings in organizational behavior and human performance.* Homewood, Ill.: Dorsey, 1969, pb.

Davis, Keith, and Scott, W. (Eds.) *Readings in human relations.* (2nd

FIGURE 7.1. Bell, J.E. A Guide to Library Research in Psychology, pp. ix, 127.

Kepner,
... ...nal manager, A...
Telberg, I. Who's who in Soviet social sciences, humanities, art and government, A329
TELEVISION
 educational aspects, H269, H288: literature reviews, H397
→ social effects: bibliography, E271–E273
Television and social behavior; an annotated bibliography on research, focussing on television's impact on children, C. K. Atkin, E272
Teller, J. D. and Good, H. G. A history of western education, H61
Temin, P. The Jacksonian econ...

buque, ... Kendall/Hunt, 1971 [...]. **(E270).**

SPECIALIZED

E271 United Nations Education, Scientific and Cultural Organization. The effects of television on children and adolescents; an annotated bibliography, with an introductory overview of research results, prepared by the International Association for Mass Communication Research. Ed. by Wilbur Schramm. Amsterdam and Paris: UNESCO, 1965. 54p.

Marks a fresh advance in codifying research.

Closely related, with later material, is Charles K. Atkin and others, *Television and social behavior; an annotated bibliography on research, focussing on television's impact on children* (Rockville, Md.: National Institute of Mental Health, 1971 [150p.]) **(E272)**. It has 550 research studies deemed significant from the standpoint of the Surgeon General's Scientific Advisory Committee on Television and Social Behavior, and annotates about 300 of the most important titles. Beno Sternberg, *Aspects sociaux de la radio et de la télévision; revue des recherches significatives, 1950–1964, avec un avant-propos d'Edgar Morin* (Paris: Mouton, 1966 [138p.]) **(E273)**, offers a broad review of the social significance of these two powerful instruments, followed by an

FIGURE 7.2. White, C.M. Sources of Information in the Social Sciences, pp. 686, 280.

Handbooks

American handbook of psychiatry. Silvano Arieti, ed.-in-chief. 2d ed. N.Y., Basic Books, 1974–75. 6v. $169.50.
EH9

Previous ed. 1959–60 in 3v. (*Guide* EH59).
Contents: v.1, The foundation of psychiatry; v.2, Child and adolescent psychiatry, sociocultural and community psychiatry; v.3, Adult clinical psychiatry; v.4, Organic disorders and psychosomatic medicine; v.5, Treatment; v.6, New psychiatric frontiers.
The *Handbook* has been completely revised, updated, and expanded. RC435.A562

Handbook of industrial and organizational psychology. Marvin D. Dunnette, ed. Chicago, Rand McNally, [1976]. 1740p. $49.95.
EH10

Contents: pt.1, Theoretical and methodological foundations of industrial and organizational psychology; pt.2, Individual and job measurement and the management of individual behavior in organizations; pt.3, Description and measurement of organizations and of behavioral processes in organizations.
"... the plan is to produce a *Handbook* that is broad in scope, giving strong emphases to both conceptual and methodological issues relevant to the study of industrial and organizational behavior."—*Pref.* Contains 37 signed chapters; most include references. Subject index. HF5548.8.H355

Handbook of parapsychology. Ed. by Benjamin B. Wolman. N.Y., Van Nostrand Reinhold, [1977]. 967p. $35. EH11

Contains 34 signed chapters on various aspects of parapsychology, all with extensive lists of references, followed by a list of suggested readings and a glossary. The chapters range from balanced treatments of research methods to some highly credulous chapters on alleged phenomena. Useful for references to the enormous recent literature. Indexed. BF1031.H254

Directories

U.S. National Institute of Mental Health. Mental health directory. Wash., Govt. Prt. Off., 1977. (DHEW publ. no. (ADM) 77-266) $7.
EH12

First publ. 1964.
"NIMH has provided listings of treatment resources in every State and Territory ... gathered from the Division's 1976 inventory of mental health facilities.... The Institute's National Clearinghouse for Mental Health Information has supplemented this material with information about Regional, State, and voluntary mental health agencies as well as mental health-related resources in other Federal agencies and in professional and private organizations."—*Pref.* Entries are arranged by state, then city, town, or county. Data include name, address, phone number, and services provided.

Style manuals

American Psychological Association. Publication manual. 2d ed. [Wash., Amer. Psychological Assoc., 1974] 136p. $5 pa.
EH13

1st ed. publ. as v.49, no.4, pt.2 (July 1952) of *Psychological bulletin.*
"This *Publication Manual* draws its rules from a large body of psychological literature, from editors and authors experienced in psychological writing, and from recognized authorities on publication practices. Writers who employ this Manual conscientiously will express their ideas in a form and style both accepted by and familiar to a broad readership in psychology."—*Introd.* BF76.7.A46

FIGURE 7.3. Sheehy, Eugene P. Guide to Reference Books, 9th edition: Supplement, p. 227.

8 Using Other Libraries

> "If we value the pursuit of knowledge, we must be free to follow wherever that search may lead us."
> — Adlai Stevenson, speech. University of Wisconsin, Madison, Oct. 8, 1952.

It is satisfying to use bibliographies, periodical indexes, and abstracts, when they lead you to vital books and articles in your library. However, these reference sources can also be frustrating if, after locating some choice items, you find that your library does not own them. This happens to students and faculty even at the largest libraries. Fortunately, the problem is not without solution *if* you act in time.

How to Request Materials from Other Libraries

Your reference librarian may be able to borrow the books you need from another library and may be able to get you photocopies of any articles you need. All the librarian needs is time, a full and accurate citation, and, in the case of photocopying, usually some cash. The time required varies from a few days to a few months, depending on whether your library is part of a cooperating network of libraries and whether the material is available in the library where it is requested. An average wait is about two weeks. The information generally required includes a full citation and identification of the place where you found the book or article cited. This may seem like bureaucratic red tape, but this information is required by lending libraries and is good insurance against errors in transmission. If you do not have the full bibliographic information, ask your reference librarian to help you find it. Libraries often make no charge for mailing books, but they seldom mail periodicals. The cost of photocopies is usually ten cents or more per exposure.

If you are an undergraduate at a university, you may find that this interlibrary loan service is not available to you; a university library serving doctoral students is presumed to have a collection that is adequate for undergraduates. Interlibrary loan service is more readily available to undergraduates at colleges, which often have made special arrangements to borrow from a nearby university or state library.

Visiting Another Library

If a large university library is close, your time is short, or your library will not borrow for you, then you may prefer to visit another library. Your reference librarian can give you the address, phone number, subject specialties, and perhaps the hours of most libraries you may want to visit. You might ask which are closest and whether you will need a pass or letter of introduction in order to use the library. Most libraries let visitors use materials in the library only.

If you need a particular periodical, your reference librarian can help you find which nearby libraries own it by using *New Serial Titles* (Washington, DC: Library of Congress, 1953–) or state and regional lists which might exist for your area. Books are a little harder to locate, but the *National Union Catalog* (Washington, DC: Library of Congress, 1953–) does give the location of a good many books. Also, there are two computer systems which can provide location information for both periodicals and books: OCLC (*O*n-line *C*omputer *L*ibrary *C*enter) and RLIN (*R*esearch *L*ibrary *I*nformation *N*etwork). Each system has a database consisting of catalog records, with information very much like that in a card catalog. Many libraries are now members of one of these networks, and your librarian can search the database to determine which other member libraries have the title you need. In some libraries there are public terminals and instructions for their use so you can perform the search yourself. Remember, though, that libraries generally have materials that do not show up in the database, since most libraries have been members of the computer networks for fewer than ten years and do not have their earlier materials in the database. Also, the fact that a library owns an item does not mean that the item will be available for your use. If only a particular title will satisfy your needs, you may want to phone a library and ask them to hold it for you if they find it on the shelf. Since most big libraries need an hour or more to look in their catalogs and on their shelves, they will probably ask you to call back.

Using the Library of Congress Subject Catalog

If you are having difficulty finding enough books on your topic, consult the subject-arranged book catalog of the world's largest library, the Library of Congress. The Library of Congress' *Subject Catalog*, previously entitled *Books: Subjects; A Cumulative List of Works Represented by Library of Congress Printed Cards*, (Washington, DC: Library of Congress, 1955–) with its annual and five-year cumulations and quarterly supplements is a subject listing of books and other material published in the U.S. from 1950 to date.

As FIGURE 8.1 shows, if you look in the 1978 volumes under the heading "Television broadcasting of news," you see that this source includes many foreign publications, such as Cheng's book, and many pamphlets, such as the 8-page European agreement. Many college libraries do not own the *Subject Catalog*, which totals over 200 volumes, but you may be able to visit a library which does have it. Any promising books you find there can be pursued through your own library and elsewhere.

When you visit another library, be sure to check its card catalog under the subject headings you found useful in your own library. The larger the psychology collection, the more you can expect to find, and you may find some useful titles you have not seen in any bibliography.

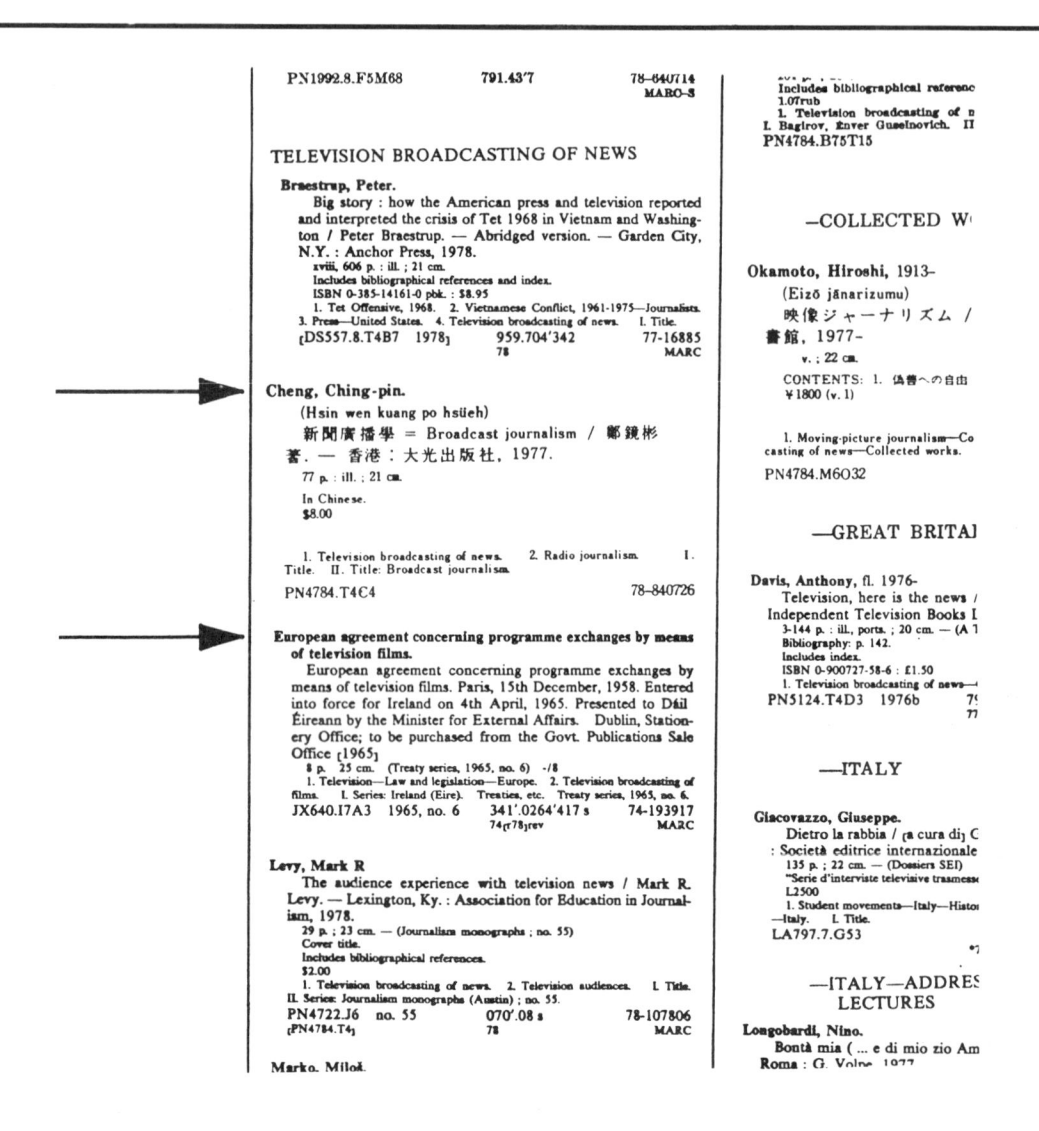

FIGURE 8.1. Library of Congress. Subject Catalog, 1978.

Summary

1. Bibliographies and periodical indexes can be frustrating to use if your library does not have the materials cited.

2. You can ask your reference librarian to borrow the books from other libraries or get photocopies of articles. Allow enough time for this procedure.

3. You can visit other libraries, with help from your reference librarian.

4. The Library of Congress' *Subject Catalog* is a comprehensive subject bibliography that can lead you to books in other libraries.

APPENDIX I

LIBRARY KNOWLEDGE TEST

PART A.

Directions: Use this catalog card to answer the questions below.

```
                The experimental analysis of behavior
BF
319     Fantino, Edmund J.
F35         The experimental analysis of behavior : a
        biological perspective / Edmund Fantino, Cheryl
        A. Logan. San Francisco : Freeman, c1979.
            xiii, 559 p. : ill. ; 24 cm. (A Series of
        books in psychology)
            Bibliography: p. 501-544.
            Includes indexes.

            1. Conditioned response. 2. Psychology,
        Experimental. 3. Psychology, Comparative.
        4. Psychobiology. I. Logan, Cheryl A.
        II. Title.
```

1. Would this card be filed with other cards beginning "T," "F," or "E"?

2. Does the book include a list of other writings?

3. Under what other headings will cards for this book be found in the catalog?

PART B.

Directions: Use this excerpt from the *Readers' Guide to Periodical Literature* to answer the following questions:

4. How do you find the full title of the periodical that has the article, "Crazy is a crazy the world around"?

5. On what page does it appear?

6. In what volume does it appear?

7. What is the date of publication?

8. Who is its author?

9. Under what heading will you find articles on "Mental telepathy"?

10. What is the purpose of listing the terms "autism" and "neuroses" under "Mental Illness"?

11. Does the article "Biochemical high-risk paradigm" include a list of other writings?

```
Pro...
    commun...              . bi.
  Fall '76
        China (People's Republic)
 Mental health in China. il Sci Digest 80:11-12
    N '76
MENTAL illness
 Biochemical high-risk paradigm: behavioral and
    familial correlates of low platelet monoamine
    oxidase activity. M. S. Buchsbaum and others.
    bibl il Science 194:339-41 O 15 '76
 Crazy is a crazy the world around; study by J.
    Murphy. J. Gaylin. Psychol Today 10:17-19 Jl
    '76
 Crazy is crazy in any language; work of Jane
    M. Murphy. Sci Digest 80:19 Jl '76
 Ingmar Bergman's next film. Face to face; ex-
    cerpt from Face to face. I. Bergman. il
    Mademoiselle 82:158-9+ Ap '76
 Psychiatric labeling in cross-cultural perspec-
    tive. J. M. Murphy. bibl il Science 191:1019-28
    Mr 12 '76
        See also
  Autism
  Neuroses
  Paranoia
  Schizophrenia
        Causes
 C-fragment of β-lipotropin: an endogenous
    neuroleptic or antipsychotogen? Y. F. Jacquet
    and N. Marks. bibl il Science 194:632-5 N 5
    '76
 Child is father to the patient—a computer profile
    of mental patients. M. Casady. Psychol Today
    10:112 N '76
 Endorphins: profound behavioral effects in rats
    suggest new etiological factors in mental ill-
    ness. F. Bloom and others. bibl il Science
    194:630-2 N 5 '76
 Environmental allergies. Sci Digest 80:15-16 O
    '76
        Prevention
 Crisis intervention theory and technique. F.
    Kaslow. bibl il Intellect 104:316-18 Ja '76
        Therapy
 Great megavitamin flap: orthomolecular psy-
    chiatry. J. Rodgers. il Sat R 3:33-6 F 21 '76
        See also
  Psychotherapy
MENTAL illness in moving pictures. See Moving
    pictures—Themes
MENTAL illness insurance. See Insurance, Health
MENTAL suggestion. See Suggestion
MENTAL telepathy. See Telepathy
MENTALLY handicapped
        See also
  Libraries—Services to the mentally handicapped
        Civil rights
 Challenge of the mentally retarded. F. K.
```

43

Answers to the Library Knowledge Test

1. "E" This is a replica of the "title card" that would be filed in the catalog under "Experimental analysis of behavior." Do not use the articles "a, an, the" as the first word when looking in the catalog. This also holds true in other languages, e.g., la, das, etc.

2. Yes, there is a bibliography on pages 501--544.

3. There will be cards filed for both authors, Fantino and Logar, and for all of the subject headings: "Conditioned response," "Psychology, Experimental," "Psychology, Comparative," and "Psychobiology."

4. Look at the list of periodical abbreviations at the front of the volume. Most indexes have such a list which decodes the abbreviated titles used in the index. In this case, the title is *Psychol(ogy) Today*; others shown in this sample are *Sci(ence) Digest* and *Sat(urday) R(eview)*.

5. Pages 17–19.

6. Volume 10.

7. July, 1976.

8. J. Gaylin.

9. Telepathy.

10. These are "see also" references relevant to "Mental illness," that is, other headings under which related articles are listed in this issue of *Readers' Guide*.

11. Yes, the abbreviation "bibl" in the citation indicates that the article includes a bibliography.

APPENDIX II

USING INDEX MEDICUS

What Is Index Medicus?

Index Medicus (Washington, DC: National Library of Medicine, 1960–) is an index which covers the literature of the biomedical sciences. Its primary users are practicing physicians and biomedical researchers. However, the range of material it indexes is not restricted to the biomedical field. Among the approximately 2,400 journals and selected monographs indexed by this service are many in the fields of psychology and sociology, as well as in such areas as botany, chemistry, entomology, veterinary medicine, and zoology. It can therefore prove to be a very useful index for psychological research, especially in those areas of psychology which are closely related to psychiatry or neurology. If *Index Medicus* is available in your library, it might be worthwhile to consult as a supplement to your search. (NOTE: Some libraries subscribe to the *Abridged Index Medicus* which indexes only 100 English language journals and is specifically designed to meet the needs of practicing physicians. This limited index would not be very useful to you.)

How to Use Index Medicus

Index Medicus is published every month and cumulated annually in the *Cumulated Index Medicus*. Both the monthly and annual issues consist of a subject index and an author index. Full bibliographical information for the documents cited is listed in both the author and subject indexes. In the author index, this information is listed only under the name of the major author, with cross-references from the other authors (FIGURE II.1).

Before using the subject index part of *Index Medicus*, it is a good idea to consult *Medical Subject Headings*, which is comparable to the *Thesaurus of Psychological Index Terms* which was described in relation to *Psychological Abstracts* (Chapter 4). *Medical Subject Headings* is divided into two parts: the "Alphabetical List" and the "Tree Structures." FIGURE II.2 illustrates a portion of the "Alphabetical List." The terms in boldface type are accepted subject headings which can be looked up in the subject index. Under the boldface terms are cross-references to related terms, notes about terms which have been replaced, and alpha-numeric codes for use in the "Tree Structures" section.

The "Tree Structures" section of *Medical Subject Headings* organizes the subject headings used in *Index Medicus* into broad categories, showing the relationships between terms. FIGURE II.3 outlines some of the categories used in the "Tree Structures," and FIGURE II.4 shows a set of related terms within category F. All of category F is psychological in nature, covering four broad areas: "Behavior and Behavior Mechanisms," "Psychological Processes and Principles," "Behavioral and Mental Disorders," and "Disciplines Behavior Tests, Therapies, Services." Each heading shown in the "Tree Structures" can be used as a term to search in the subject index of *Index Medicus*, so browsing through the "Tree Structures" is a good use of your time before using the subject index.

"Psychology" can also be used as a subdivision for the subject headings in four other categories of headings in *Index Medicus*: Group C (Diseases), Group E1–6 (Pro-

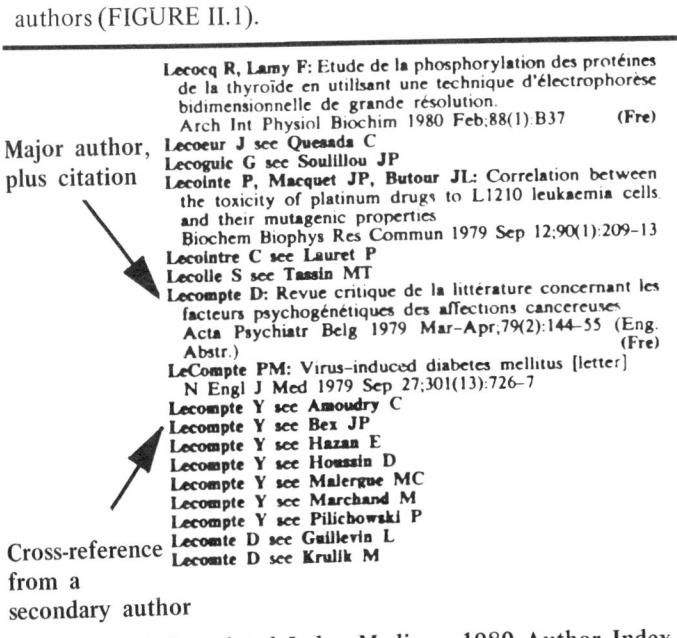

FIGURE II.1 Cumulated Index Medicus, 1980 Author Index.

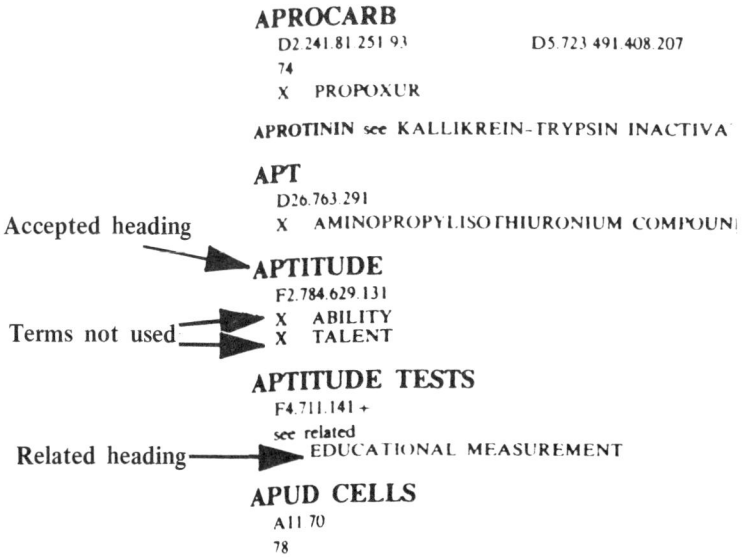

FIGURE II.2 Medical Subject Headings, 1980. "Alphabetical List."

E6	Dentistry	769
E7	Equipment and Supplies	772

F Psychiatry and Psychology

F1	Behavior and Behavior Mechanisms	774
F2	Psychological Processes and Principles	779
F3	Behavioral and Mental Disorders	783
F4	Disciplines, Tests, Therapy, Services	788

G Biological Sciences

G1	Biological Sciences	791
G2	Health Occupations	792
G3	Environment and Public Health	795
G4	Biological Phenomena, Cell Physiology, Immunity	799

FIGURE II.3 Medical Subject Headings, 1980. Categories and subcategories.

cedures and Technics), Group F3 (Behavioral and Mental Disorders), and Group M (Named Groups, such as Blacks, Jews, Parents, Women, Students, etc.). FIGURE II.5 illustrates a section of the 1980 subject index with the main heading "Neoplasms" (from Group C) and the subheading "Psychology." Because the article cited here is not in English, its translated title is placed in brackets and the original language is indicated by a three-letter code in parentheses following the citation. In addition, we are told that there is an English abstract of the article in the issue of the journal in which it appears. In the author index, only the original language title of the article is given (FIGURE II.1).

Conclusion

Because of the psychological categories included in its indexing terminology and the use of "Psychology" as a standard subheading, *Index Medicus* is a very useful supplemental index for psychological research. The subject index is not very difficult to use, but to use it effectively you must learn how to use *Medical Subject Headings*. Although you might need the help of a reference librarian when you first try to use *Medical Subject Headings*, you will find that the effort needed to learn how to use it properly will be rewarded by an improved retrieval of relevant articles from *Index Medicus*.

UNCONSCIOUS (PSYCHOLOGY)	F2.739.794.942	F1.752.747.	
PSYCHOLOGY, APPLIED	F2.784		
COUNSELING	F2.784.176	F4.408.413	N2.421.14
PASTORAL CARE	F2.784.176.560	F2.880.410	
CRIMINAL PSYCHOLOGY	F2.784.240		
LIE DETECTION	F2.784.240.514	F2.830.512	I1.198.560
HUMAN ENGINEERING	F2.784.412	J1.293.556	
DATA DISPLAY	F2.784.412.221	L1.382.460	
MAN-MACHINE SYSTEMS	F2.784.412.575	J1.293.556.	J1.897.441
TASK PERFORMANCE AND ANALYSIS	F2.784.412.846	F2.523.696	F2.784.692
TIME AND MOTION STUDIES ·	F2.784.412.846.707	F2.784.692.	J1.293.556
PSYCHOLOGY, EDUCATIONAL	F2.784.629	F4.96.628.	
ACHIEVEMENT	F2.784.629.54	F1.658.59	
➤ APTITUDE	➤ F2.784.629.131		
ASPIRATIONS (PSYCHOLOGY)	F2.784.629.155	F1.658.100	
CHILD, EXCEPTIONAL	F2.784.629.228	M1.471.392.	
CHILD, GIFTED	F2.784.629.228.350	M1.471.392.	
CHILD GUIDANCE	F2.784.629.272	F4.408.192	
EDUCATION OF MENTALLY RETARDED	F2.784.629.375	I2.233.213.	
LEARNING	F2.784.629.529	F2.463.425	
REMEDIAL TEACHING	F2.784.629.709	I2.903.694	
STUDENT DROPOUTS	F2.784.629.796	I2.233.748.	M1.848.60
UNDERACHIEVEMENT	F2.784.629.880		
VOCATIONAL GUIDANCE	F2.784.629.937	F2.784.692.	I2.233.924
PSYCHOLOGY, INDUSTRIAL	F2.784.692	F4.96.628.	
ABSENTEEISM	F2.784.692.107	J1.750.180	
EFFICIENCY	F2.784.692.351		

FIGURE II.4 Medical Subject Headings, 1980. "Tree structures."

Main heading ⟶ **NEOPLASMS**

Abstr.) (Pol)
[Malignant neoplasm morbidity in the population of the RSFSR during 12 years (1966-1977)] Kozlova EV, et al. **Sov Med** 1979 Nov;(11):90-3 (Rus)
[Character of the dynamics and prediction of probable levels of malignant neoplasm morbidity among the population of the USSR] Merabishvili VM. **Sov Zdravookhr** 1979;(7):30-3 (Eng. Abstr.) (Rus)
[Ethnic aspects of cancer distribution in Dagestan] Aliev RG. **Vopr Onkol** 1980;26(1):87-90 (Eng. Abstr.) (Rus)
[Malignant neoplasm morbidity among the population of the USSR in 1976] Napalkov NP, et al. **Vopr Onkol** 1980; 26(4):10-43 (Rus)
[Peculiarities of malignant neoplasm morbidity among the population of the USSR in 1977] Napalkov NP, et al. **Vopr Onkol** 1980;26(4):43-62 (Rus)
[Tumors in children] Pokk LR. **Vopr Onkol** 1979;25(7):83-6 (Eng. Abstr.) (Rus)
[Geographic pathology of cancer and registry of tumor pathology] Rolón PA. **Bol Of Sanit Panam** 1979 Sep; 87(3):232-7 (Eng. Abstr.) (Spa)
[How common is occupational cancer?] Ahlmark A, et al. **Lakartidningen** 1979 Aug 29;76(35):2895-8 (Swe)
[Characteristics of the distribution of malignant tumors among the children of the Carpathian region] Hodovanets' BI, et al. **Pediatr Akush Ginekol** 1979 Jul-Aug;(4):23-4 (Ukr)

Sub-headings ⟶ **PATHOLOGY**

Bone marrow biopsy in patients with malignant neoplasms other than lymphomas or leukemia. Cohen Y, et al. **Acta Haematol (Basel)** 1979;62(4):181-4
Aging, cancer and cell membranes. Based on a series of lectures presented at the Given Institute of Pathobiology of the University of Colorado in Aspen, Colorado, August 1978. **Adv Pathobiol** 1980;7:1-395
Fine-needle aspiration cytology. Colón VF, et al. **Am Fam Physician** 1980 Jun;21(6):89-93
Percutaneous asp... Betsill WL Jr, et al.

...ons] Berzin ...
...0 (Eng. Abstr.) (Rus)
... prevention center in Ukraine] Pozmogov AI, et al. **Vopr Onkol** 1980;26(7):105-7 (Rus)

PSYCHOLOGY

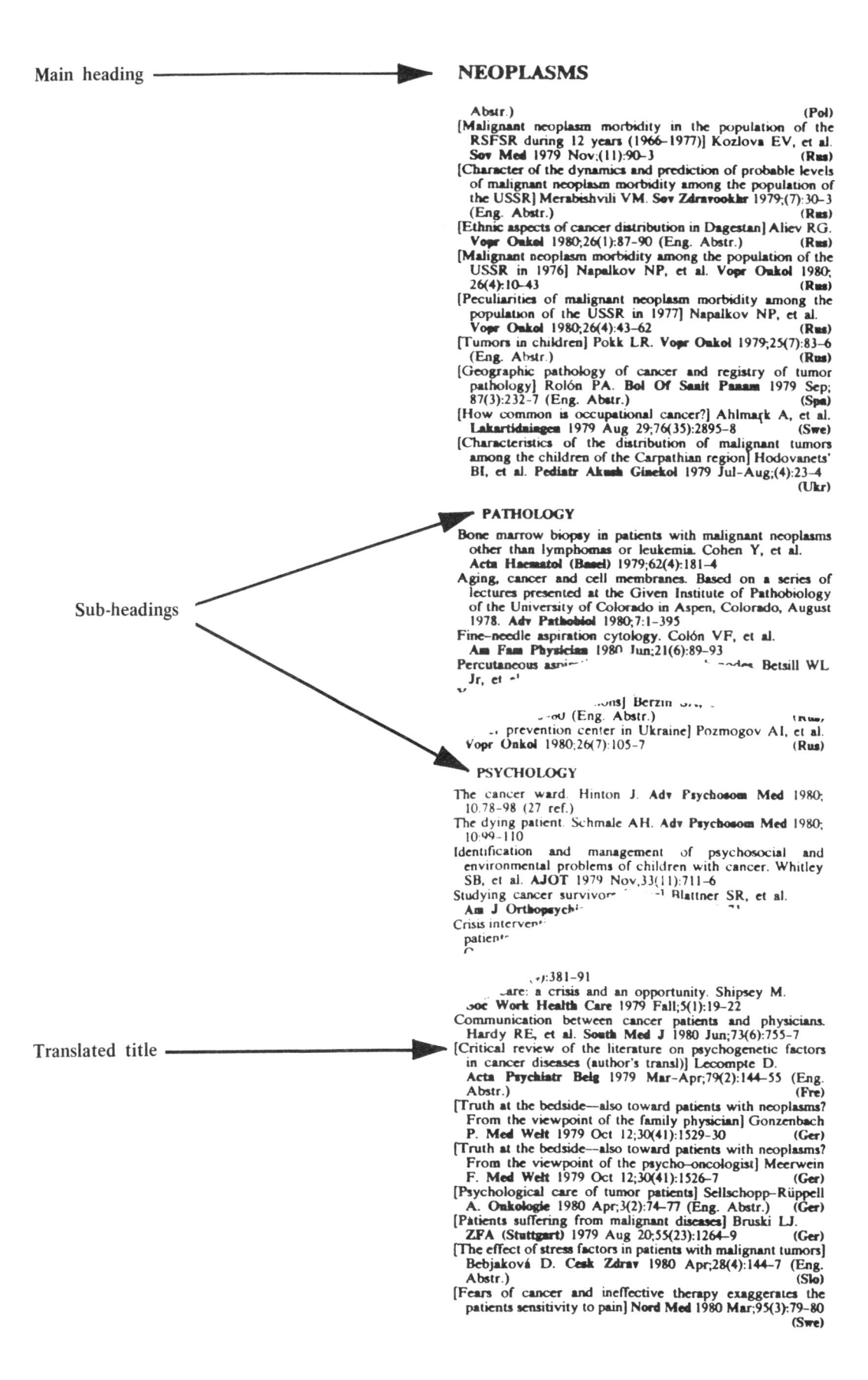

The cancer ward. Hinton J. **Adv Psychosom Med** 1980; 10:78-98 (27 ref.)
The dying patient. Schmale AH. **Adv Psychosom Med** 1980; 10:99-110
Identification and management of psychosocial and environmental problems of children with cancer. Whitley SB, et al. **AJOT** 1979 Nov;33(11):711-6
Studying cancer survivor... Blattner SR, et al. **Am J Orthopsych...**
Crisis interven...
patien...

...):381-91
...are: a crisis and an opportunity. Shipsey M. **Soc Work Health Care** 1979 Fall;5(1):19-22
Communication between cancer patients and physicians. Hardy RE, et al. **South Med J** 1980 Jun;73(6):755-7

Translated title ⟶ [Critical review of the literature on psychogenetic factors in cancer diseases (author's transl)] Lecompte D. **Acta Psychiatr Belg** 1979 Mar-Apr;79(2):144-55 (Eng. Abstr.) (Fre)
[Truth at the bedside—also toward patients with neoplasms? From the viewpoint of the family physician] Gonzenbach P. **Med Welt** 1979 Oct 12;30(41):1529-30 (Ger)
[Truth at the bedside—also toward patients with neoplasms? From the viewpoint of the psycho-oncologist] Meerwein F. **Med Welt** 1979 Oct 12;30(41):1526-7 (Ger)
[Psychological care of tumor patients] Sellschopp-Rüppell A. **Onkologie** 1980 Apr;3(2):74-77 (Eng. Abstr.) (Ger)
[Patients suffering from malignant diseases] Bruski LJ. **ZFA (Stuttgart)** 1979 Aug 20;55(23):1264-9 (Ger)
[The effect of stress factors in patients with malignant tumors] Bebjaková D. **Cesk Zdrav** 1980 Apr;28(4):144-7 (Eng. Abstr.) (Slo)
[Fears of cancer and ineffective therapy exaggerates the patients sensitivity to pain] **Nord Med** 1980 Mar;95(3):79-80 (Swe)

FIGURE II.5 Cumulated Index Medicus, 1980, Subject Index.

APPENDIX III

USING THE MONTHLY CATALOG OF
UNITED STATES GOVERNMENT PUBLICATIONS

The United States Government Printing Office (G.P.O.) is the world's largest publisher. It publishes documents ranging in size from one page to many volumes which are issued by the various departments of the government and by Congress and its myriad committees and subcommittees. Many of these government bodies, such as the National Institute of Mental Health, the National Institute on Alcohol Abuse and Alcoholism, and the National Institute on Drug Abuse, regularly publish material relevant to research in psychology. In addition, hearings held before Congressional committees such as the House or Senate Special Committees on Aging, often contain testimony presented by experts on topics of current interest. The various government agencies also publish a wide range of statistical and demographic information which can be very useful for certain types of psychological studies. A comprehensive psychology research strategy should include government publications, and this is especially true if you have access to a library which is a complete or partial U.S. government depository library. Such libraries automatically receive all or a selected part of the documents published by the G.P.O. and are required by law to make them available to the public.

Usually you should consult the sources listed in the main part of this book before looking specifically for government documents. However, in certain areas of research, you might want to explore government documents early in your information search. For instance, if your topic is somewhat controversial or of current interest, you might be able to find some useful Congressional committee hearings which present the issue and expert testimony supporting different points of view. Often government publications will provide background summaries of an issue which can be very useful in the initial stages of your research, and the government is an excellent source of statistical or demographic data. To find out what documents are available on the subject you are researching, you will have to consult the *Monthly Catalog of United States Government Publications* (Washington, DC: U.S. Government Printing Office, 1895–).

The *Monthly Catalog* has undergone numerous changes in title and format since it was first published in the nineteenth century. The most recent major changes occurred with the publication of the July 1976 issue of the *Monthly Catalog*. The information contained in this chapter is applicable to the *Monthly Catalog* format from that issue to the present.

In each monthly issue the *Monthly Catalog* lists documents published by the G.P.O., in an arrangement based on government departments. Thus, a typical issue of the *Monthly Catalog* will list first the publications of the Agriculture Department and its various divisions (e.g., Forest Service, Soil Conservation Service), then the Commerce Department and its divisions (Census Bureau, etc.), and so on through the

grap... ...ciated equip...
3883

Television — Receivers and reception — Testing.
Characterization of electrical ignition sources within television receivers /, 80-2116

Television and children.
Address by the Honorable Richard E. Wiley, Chairman, Federal Communications Commission before the National Association of Secondary School Principals, Washington, D.C., February 16, 1976., 80-7198 ◄──── entry number
Children and television /, 80-2729

Television and youth.
Address by the Honorable Richard E. Wiley, Chairman, Federal Communications Commission before the National Association of Secondary School Principals, Washington, D.C., February 16, 1976., 80-7198

Television broadcasting — United States.
First report on prospects for additional networks 80-2370o

FIGURE III.1 Monthly Catalog, 1980 Cumulative subject index.

Superintendent of Documents number
Entry number

80-7198   CC 1.15:W 64
Wiley, Richard E.
  Address by the Honorable Richard E. Wiley, Chairman, Federal Communications Commission before the National Association of Secondary School Principals, Washington, D.C., February 16, 1976. — Washington : The Commission, [1976?]
20554
  11 p. ; 27 cm.
  Caption title: Violence, the media and the school.
  "61156."
  pbk.
  1. Television and youth. 2. Television and children. 3. Violence in television. I. United States. Federal Communications Commission. II. National Association of Secondary School Principals. III. Title. IV. Title: Violence, the media and the school.
OCLC 5962287

Subject headings

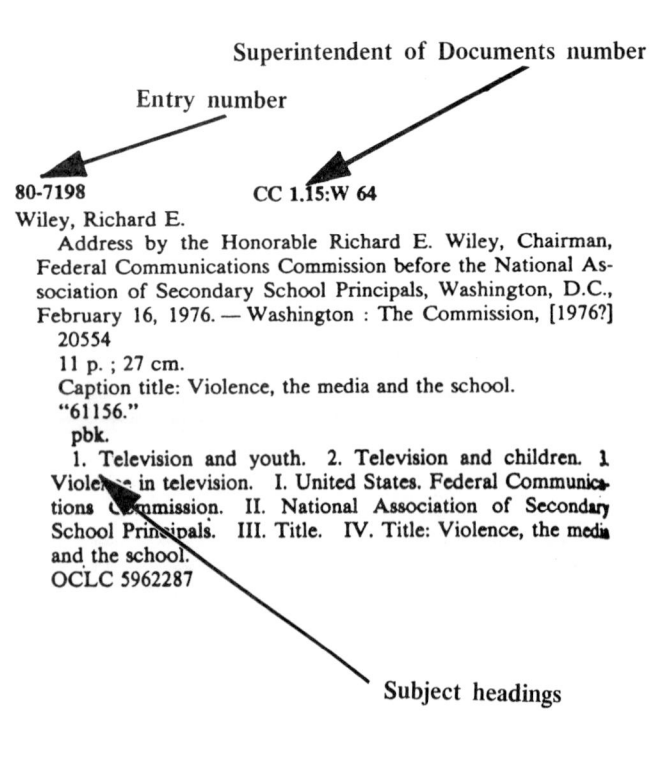

FIGURE III.2 Monthly Catalog, April–June 1980.

alphabet to the publications of the Veterans Administration. After these items, there is a section which lists the publications of Congress and its committees and subcommittees. The final section of each issue contains six indexes to the documents listed: Author, Title, Subject, Series/Report Number, Stock Number, and Title Key Word (this last index was begun on a trial basis with the July 1980 issue of the *Monthly Catalog*). In this chapter, we will only be concerned with the Subject and Title Key Word indexes — the others are not as useful for your research needs in most cases.

The Subject Index in the *Monthly Catalog* uses the same vocabulary as the *Library of Congress Subject Headings* (see Chapter 2), with some terms added. FIGURE III.1 shows a section from the January-June 1980 semiannual cumulation of the *Monthly Catalog* Subject Index. Under the heading "Television and children," two titles are listed. The first title ends with the number 80-7198. This number is the key to finding a more complete description of the document. Each document description in the *Monthly Catalog* is given a unique, sequential number, and 80-7198 is the 7198th document listed in the *1980* issues of the *Monthly Catalog*. The document number functions in much the same manner as the abstract number in indexes of *Psychological Abstracts*. The document description itself, shown in FIGURE III.2, is very similar in content and format to a library catalog card. One significant difference is the number in boldface type at the top center of the entry (CC 1.15:W 64). This is the Superintendent of Documents Number, which is used by most government documents collections as a call number for arranging documents on the shelves. Some libraries use different call number systems, however, so check with your reference or documents librarian before trying to find documents. Notice, too, that the subject headings assigned to this document are listed at the bottom of the entry. You should look for subject headings which you have not yet used. For example, if you have not looked up "Violence in television," its presence as the third subject heading listed for document 80-7198 should alert you to the need for doing so.

The Title Key Word Index also provides subject access to the documents listed in the *Monthly Catalog*. Like the "Permuterm Index" of the *Social Sciences Citation Index* (see Chapter 5), this index is based on the significant words in the titles of the documents listed. It is especially useful if you are interested in a very specific or new topic which would be hard to find using the subject approach only. However, it is wise to use the Key Word Index in conjunction with the Subject Index, not instead of it. For example, the document described in FIGURE III.2 could not have been found using the Key Word Index because the word "television" does not appear in its title. FIGURE III.3 shows a section of the Title Key Word Index from the January-June 1980 semiannual cumulation.

Conclusion

Most thorough search strategies should include an attempt to glean relevant information from the huge number of documents issued by the United States Government. The *Monthly Catalog of United States Government Publications* will lead you to timely and authoritative material relevant to your topic, and it will provide you with information not likely to be duplicated in the other sources you use.

In addition to the *Monthly Catalog*, there are several other indexes which can be used to locate government publications. Some of these are listed in Appendix IV.

	80-20750
typewriter repairer /	80-11717
" repairer /	80-11718
" repairer /	80-11719
television /, Children and	80-2729
" actions., Public notice - Federal Commu	80-558
" actions, Cable	80-558
" and performance rights :, Copyright iss	80-19488
" antenna performance /, Indoor	80-7180
" authorization actions., Public notice -	80-559
" authorization actions, Cable	80-559
" certificate of compliance actions., Pub	80-562
" certificate of compliance actions, Cabl	80-562
" from the Senate floor /	80-13335
" program production, acquisition, and di	80-23701
" programs., Radio and	80-12589
" receivers /, Characterization of electr	80-2116
" receivers, phonographs, and related equ	80-3883
" relay service (CARS) applications., Pub	80-561
" relay service (CARS) applications, Cabl	80-561
" service applications., Public notice -	80-560
" service applications, Cable	80-560
" systems /, A guide to technical standar	80-25190
" systems specialist /, Radio/	80-18043
" systems specialist /, Radio/	80-18044
" systems specialist /, Radio/	80-18045
" ., Media arts: film, radio,	80-10661
television-cable installer., The US Army Signal Sc	80-4167
teliospores by single aeciospore lines of Cronarti	80-25069

FIGURE III.3 Monthly Catalog, 1980.
Cumulative title key word index.

APPENDIX IV

BASIC REFERENCE SOURCES FOR PSYCHOLOGY COURSES

The first library search with any of the following course-related bibliographies will be easier if used with the main body of the book, or in conjunction with Appendix V, "Guidelines for Proceeding." Most of the work on this bibliography was done in 1980. It has been updated as much as time allowed by adding appropriate new titles reviewed in *American Reference Books Annual* through 1981, and *Contemporary Psychology* through the 1981 issues. The newest editions were verified for each title.

Because there is often overlap in subject matter between psychology courses, cross-references have been included in the outline of courses below. An asterisk precedes titles explained in the text of this book.

Outline of Classified Bibliography

I. General Psychology Reference Sources

    A. Encyclopedias, Handbooks
    B. Dictionaries
    C. Review Serials, Yearbooks
    D. Periodical Indexes, Abstracting Services
    E. Bibliographies
    F. Bibliographies of Serials
    G. Bibliographies of Bibliographies
    H. Book Reviews
    I. Biographies, Directories
    J. Indexes to Government Publications
    K. Guides to the Literature of Psychology
    L. Handbooks for Writing Psychology Papers

II. Abnormal Psychology, Psychiatry, Psychoanalysis (see also III, IV, VIII, XI)

    A. Encyclopedias, Handbooks
    B. Dictionaries
    C. Review Serials, Yearbooks
    D. Periodical Indexes, Abstracting Services
    E. Bibliographies
    F. Directory

III. Behavior (see also II, IV, VI)

    A. Encyclopedias, Handbooks
    B. Review Serials, Yearbooks
    C. Periodical Indexes, Abstracting Services
    D. Bibliographies

IV. Child Development, Adolescence, Retardation (see also II, III, VI, XI)

    A. Encyclopedias, Handbooks
    B. Review Serials, Yearbooks
    C. Periodical Indexes, Abstracting Services
    D. Bibliographies

V. Comparative Psychology, Animal Psychology

    A. Handbooks
    B. Review Serials, Yearbooks
    C. Periodical Indexes, Abstracting Services

VI. Educational Psychology, Motivation, Learning (see also III, IV, VIII)

    A. Encyclopedias, Handbooks
    B. Dictionaries
    C. Review Serials
    D. Periodical Indexes, Abstracting Services
    E. Bibliographies

VII. Experimental Psychology, Research Techniques, Statistics (see also XVI)

    A. Handbooks
    B. Dictionaries

VIII. Guidance, Counselling, Communication, Psychology and Religion (see also II, IV, VI)

    A. Handbooks
    B. Review Serials, Yearbooks
    C. Periodical Indexes, Abstracting Services
    D. Bibliographies

IX. History and Systems of Psychology

X. Parapsychology

    A. Encyclopedias, Handbooks
    B. Bibliographies

XI. Personality (see also II, IV)

    A. Handbooks
    B. Dictionaries
    C. Review Serials, Yearbooks

XII. Physiological Psychology, Senses and Sensation, Drugs (see also II, VII)

   A. Handbooks
   B. Review Serials, Yearbooks
   C. Periodical Indexes, Abstracting Services
   D. Bibliographies

XIII. Psychology of Aging (see also II)

   A. Handbooks
   B. Bibliographies

XIV. Psychology of Women

   A. Encyclopedias
   B. Abstracting Services
   C. Bibliographies

XV. Social, Industrial, Organizational Psychology

   A. Handbooks
   B. Dictionaries
   C. Review Serials, Yearbooks
   D. Periodical Indexes, Abstracting Services
   E. Bibliographies

XVI. Tests and Measurements (see also VII)

   A. Handbooks
   B. Dictionaries
   C. Review Serials

References

I. General Psychology Reference Sources

   A. Encyclopedias, Handbooks

   Deutsch, Albert and Helen Fishman, eds. *Encyclopedia of Mental Health*. New York: Watts, 1963. 6 vols.
   Eysenck, H.J., Wilhelm Arnold, and Richard Meili, eds. *Encyclopedia of Psychology*. New York: Herder and Herder, 1972. 3 vols.
   Goldenson, Robert M. *The Encyclopedia of Human Behavior; Psychology, Psychiatry and Mental Health*. Garden City, NY: Doubleday, 1970. 2 vols.
   Koch, Sigmund, ed. *Psychology, A Study of a Science*. v. 1-- . New York: McGraw-Hill, 1959-- .
   Neel, Ann Marie Filinger. *Theories of Psychology, A Handbook*. Rev. and enl. ed. Cambridge, MA: Schenkman, 1977. 699 pp.
   *Sills, David L., ed. *International Encyclopedia of the Social Sciences*. New York: Macmillan, 1968. 18 vols.
   *Wolman, Benjamin B., ed. *International Encyclopedia of Psychiatry, Psychology, Psychoanalysis & Neurology*. New York: Van Nostrand Reinhold, 1977. 12 vols.

   B. Dictionaries

   Beigel, Hugo G. *Dictionary of Psychology and Related Fields: German-English*. New York: Ungar, 1971. 256 pp.
   Chaplin, James P. *Dictionary of Psychology*. New rev. ed. New York: Dell, 1975. 576 pp.
   Drever, James. *A Dictionary of Psychology*. Rev. ed. by Harvey Wallerstein. Baltimore: Penguin, 1974. 320 pp.
   Duijker, Hubertius C.J., ed. *Trilingual Psychological Dictionary*. Paris: Masson, 1978. 3 vols.
   English, Horace B. and Ava C. English. *A Comprehensive Dictionary of Psychological and Psychoanalytical Terms: A Guide to Usage*. New York: Longmans, Green, 1958. 594 pp.
   Gould, Julius, and William L. Kolb, eds. *A Dictionary of the Social Sciences*. New York: Free Press of Glencoe, 1964. 761 pp.
   Harriman, Philip L. *Handbook of Psychological Terms*. Totowa, NJ: Littlefield, Adams, 1965. 222 pp.
   Heidenreich, Charles A. *Dictionary of General Psychology: Basic Terminology and Key Concepts*. Dubuque, IA: Kendall/Hunt, 1970. 309 pp.
   Wolman, Benjamin B., and others, eds. *Dictionary of Behavioral Science*. New York: Van Nostrand Reinhold, 1973. 478 pp.

   C. Review Serials, Yearbooks

   Annual Review of Psychology. v. 1-- . Stanford, CA: Annual Reviews, 1950-- .
   Annual Review of Sociology. v. 1-- . Stanford, CA: Annual Reviews, 1975-- .

   D. Periodical Indexes, Abstracting Services

   Catalog of Selected Documents in Psychology. v. 1-- . Washington, DC: American Psychological Association, 1971-- .
   Comprehensive Dissertation Index. v. 1-- . Ann Arbor, MI: University Microfilms International, 1973-- .
   Current Contents: Social & Behavioral Sciences. v. 1-- . Philadelphia: Institute for Scientific Information, 1974-- .
   Dissertation Abstracts International. v. 1-- . Ann Arbor, MI: University Microfilms International, 1938-- .
   Doctoral Dissertations in the Health and Behavioral Sciences. Ann Arbor, MI: University Microfilms International, 1976. 160 pp.
   Index Medicus. v. 1-- . Washington, DC: National Library of Medicine, 1960-- .

Masters Abstracts: Abstracts of Selected Masters Theses on Microfilm. v. 1– . Ann Arbor, MI: University Microfilms International, 1962– .

Philosopher's Index. Cumulative ed. 1967/68– . Bowling Green, OH: Philosophy Documentation Center, Bowling Green University, 1967– .

*Psychological Abstracts. v. 1– . Washington, DC: American Psychological Assn., 1927– .

Psychological Reader's Guide. v. 1– . Lausanne, Switzerland: Elsevier Sequoia, 1973– .

Public Affairs Information Service Bulletin. v. 1– . New York: Public Affairs Information Service, 1915– .

*Social Sciences Citation Index. 1966– . Philadelphia: Institute for Scientific Information, 1973– .

*Social Sciences Index. v. 1– . New York: H.W. Wilson, 1974– .

E. Bibliographies

L'Annee Psychologique. v. 1– . Paris: Presses universitaires de France, 1894– .

Bibiographie der Deutschsprachigen Psychologischen Literatur. v. 1– . Frankfurt am Main: Vittorio Klostermann, 1971– .

Harvard University. *Harvard List of Books in Psychology.* 4th ed. Cambridge: Harvard University Press, 1971. 108 pp.

Harvard University. Library. *Philosophy and Psychology.* Cambridge: Harvard University Press, 1973. 2 vols.

Indiana University. Institute for Sex Research. Library. *Catalog of the Social and Behavioral Sciences Monograph Section of the Library.* Boston: G.K. Hall, 1975. 4 vols.

*Monthly Catalog of United States Government Publications. v. 1– . Washington, DC: U.S. Government Printing Office, 1895– .

New York Public Library. Research Libraries. *Bibliographic Guide to Psychology.* v. 1– . Boston: G.K. Hall, 1975– .

Psychological Index, 1894–1935: An Annual Bibliography of the Literature of Psychology and Cognate Subjects. Princeton, NJ: Psychological Review Co., 1895–1936.

Quarterly Check-list of Psychology. v. 1– . Darien, CT: American Bibliographic Service, 1961– .

Recent Publications in the Social and Behavioral Sciences. v. 1– . Beverly Hills, CA: American Behavioral Scientist, 1966– .

Bibliographies of Serials

Arnold, Darlene B. and Kenneth O. Doyle. *Education/Psychology Journals: A Scholar's Guide.* Metuchen, NJ: Scarecrow Press, 1975. 143 pp.

Markle, Allan and Roger C. Rinn. *Author's Guide to Journals in Psychology, Psychiatry, & Social Work.* New York: Haworth Press, 1977. 256 pp.

Tompkins, Margaret and Norma Shirley. *Serials in Psychology and Allied Fields.* 2d ed., rev. and enl. Troy, NY: Whitston, 1976. 472 pp.

Ulrich's International Periodicals Directory. 21st ed. New York: Bowker, 1982. 2 vols.

G. Bibliographies of Bibliographies

Bibliographic Index: A Cumulative Bibliography of Bibliographies. v. 1– . New York: H.W. Wilson, 1937– .

H. Book Reviews

Book Review Digest. v. 1– . New York: H.W. Wilson, 1905– .

Book Review Index. v. 1– . Detroit: Gale Research, 1965– .

Contemporary Psychology: A Journal of Reviews. v. 1– . Washington, DC: American Psychological Association, 1956– .

Current Book Review Citations. v. 1–7. New York: H.W. Wilson, 1976–1982.

Psychological Bulletin. v. 1– . Washington, DC: American Psychological Association, 1904– .

Rzepecki, Arnold M., ed. *Book Review Index to Social Science Periodicals.* v. 1– . Ann Arbor, MI: Pierian Press, 1978– .

Social Sciences Citation Index. 1966– . Philadelphia: Institute for Scientific Information, 1973– .

I. Biographies, Directories

American Men and Women of Science: Social and Behavioral Sciences. 13th ed. New York: Bowker, 1978. 1545 pp.

Directory of the American Psychological Association. v. 1– . Washington, DC: American Psychological Association, 1978– .

Jacobson, Eugene H., Gunther Reinert, and D. Detlef Herrig, eds. *International Directory of Psychologists, Exclusive of the U.S.A.* 3d ed. Amsterdam, NY: North-Holland, 1980. 589 pp.

Wolman, Bernard B. *International Directory of Psychology: A Guide to People, Places, and Policies.* New York: Plenum, 1979. 279 pp.

J. Indexes to Government Publications

American Statistics Index: A Comprehensive Guide and Index to the Statistical Publications of the U.S. Government. v. 1– . Washington, DC: Congressional Information Service, 1973– .

CIS/Index to Publications of the United States Congress. v. 1– . Washington, DC: Congressional Information Service, 1970– .

Index to U.S. Government Periodicals. v. 1– . Chicago: Infordata International, 1975– .

**Monthly Catalog of United States Government Publications.* v. 1– . Washington, DC: United States Government Printing Office, 1895– .

K. Guides to the Literature of Psychology

*Bell, James E. *A Guide to Library Research in Psychology.* Dubuque, IA: W.C. Brown, 1971. 211 pp.

Elliot, Charles K. *A Guide to the Documentation of Psychology.* Hamden, CT: Linnet Books, 1971. 134 pp.

Freides, Thelma. *Literature and Bibliography of the Social Sciences.* Los Angeles: Melville, 1973. 284 pp.

Gottsegen, Gloria B. and Abby J. Gottsegen. *Humanistic Psychology: A Guide to Information Sources.* Detroit: Gale Research Co., 1980. 185 pp.

Hoselitz, Bert F., ed. *A Reader's Guide to the Social Sciences.* Rev. ed. New York: Free Press, 1972. 425 pp.

Li, Tze-chung. *Social Science Reference Sources: A Practical Guide.* Westport, CT: Greenwood Press, 1980. 315 pp.

Sarbin, Theodore R. and William C. Coe. *The Student Psychologist's Handbook: A Guide to Sources.* Cambridge, MA: Schenkman, 1969. 104 pp.

*White, Carl M. *Sources of Information in the Social Sciences: A Guide to the Literature.* 2d ed. Chicago: American Library Association, 1973. 702 pp.

L. Handbooks for Writing Psychology Papers

*American Psychological Association. *Publication Manual of the American Psychological Association.* 2d ed. Washington, DC: American Psychological Association, 1974. 136 pp.

Mullins, Carolyn J. *A Guide to Writing and Publishing in the Social and Behavioral Sciences.* New York: Wiley, 1977. 431 pp.

Sternberg, Robert J. *Writing the Psychology Paper.* Woodbury, NY: Barron's, 1977. 243 pp.

II. Abnormal Psychology, Psychiatry, Psychoanalysis

A. Encyclopedias, Handbooks

Arieti, Silvano, ed. *American Handbook of Psychiatry.* 2d ed. New York: Basic Books, 1974–75. 6 vols.

Corsini, Raymond J. *Handbook of Innovative Psychotherapies.* New York: Wiley, 1981. 969 pp.

Eidelberg, Ludwig, ed. *Encyclopedia of Psychoanalysis.* New York: Free Press, 1968. 571 pp.

Eysenck, Hans J. *Handbook of Abnormal Psychology.* 2d ed. San Diego: Knapp, 1973. 906 pp.

Garfield, Sol L. and Allen E. Bergin, eds. *Handbook of Psychotherapy and Behavior Change: An Empirical Analysis.* 2d ed. New York: Wiley, 1978. 1024 pp.

Gurman, Alan S. and David P. Knishern, eds. *Handbook of Family Therapy.* New York: Brunner/Mazel, 1981. 796 pp.

Krauss, Stephen. *Encyclopaedic Handbook of Medical Psychology.* London: Butterworths, 1976. 585 pp.

Leigh, Denis, C.M.B. Pare and John Marks. *A Concise Encyclopedia of Psychiatry.* Baltimore: University Park Press, 1977. 399 pp.

Milt, Harry. *Basic Handbook on Mental Illness.* 3d ed., rev. and enl. Maplewood, NJ: Scientific Aids Publications, 1976. 126 pp.

Nicholi, Armand M., Jr., ed. *The Harvard Guide to Modern Psychiatry.* Cambridge, MA: Belknap Press of Harvard University Press, 1978. 681 pp.

Solomon, Philip and Veron D. Patch, eds. *Handbook of Psychiatry.* 3d ed. Los Altos, CA: Lange Medical Publications, 1974. 705 pp.

Wolman, Benjamin B. *Handbook of Clinical Psychology.* New York: McGraw-Hill, 1965. 1596 pp.

Woody, Robert H. *Encyclopedia of Clinical Assessment.* San Francisco: Jossey-Bass, 1980. 2 vols.

B. Dictionaries

American Psychiatric Association. *A Psychiatric Glossary.* 5th ed. Washington: American Psychiatric Association, 1980. 142 pp.

Brussel, James A. and George L. Cantzlaar. *The Layman's Dictionary of Psychiatry.* New York: Barnes & Noble, 1967. 269 pp.

Campbell, Robert J. *Psychiatric Dictionary.* 5th ed. New York: Oxford University Press, 1981. 693 pp.

Fann, William E. and Charles E. Goshen. *The Language of Mental Health.* 2d ed. St. Louis: Mosby, 1977. 165 pp.

Rycroft, Charles. *A Critical Dictionary of Psychoanalysis.* New York: Basic Books, 1968. 189 pp.

C. Review Serials, Yearbooks

Annual of Psychoanalysis. v. 1– . New York: International Universities Press, 1973– .

Annual Review of Schizophrenic Syndrome. v. 1– . New York: Brunner/Mazel, 1971– .

Current Psychiatric Therapies. v. 1– . New York: Grune and Stratton, 1961– .

Group and Family Therapy. v. 1– . New York: Brunner/Mazel, 1980– .

Psychoanalysis and Contemporary Science: An Annual of Integrative and Interdisciplinary Studies. v. 1– . New York: International Universities Press, 1972– .

Recent Advances in Biological Psychiatry. v. 1– . New York: Plenum, 1962– .

**Yearbook of Psychiatry and Applied Mental Health.* v. 1– . Chicago: Year Book Medical Publishers, 1970– .

D. Periodical Indexes, Abstracting Services

*Index Medicus. v. 1– . Washington, DC: National Library of Medicine, 1960– .

Science Citation Index. v. 1– . Philadelphia: Institute for Scientific Information, 1961– .

E. Bibliographies

Chicago. Institute for Psychoanalysis. *Chicago Psychoanalytic Literature Index, 1920–1970.* Chicago: CPL, 1971.

Chicago. Institute for Psychoanalysis. *Chicago Psychoanalytic Literature Index, 1971–1974.* Chicago: CPL, 1979.

Driver, Edwin D. *The Sociology and Anthropology of Mental Sickness: A Reference Guide.* Rev. and enl. ed. Amherst: University of Massachusetts Press, 1972. 487 pp.

Ennis, B. *Guide to the Literature in Psychiatry.* Los Angeles: Partridge Press, 1971. 127 pp.

Greenberg, Bette. *How to Find Out in Psychiatry: A Guide to Sources of Mental Health Information.* New York: Pergamon, 1978. 113 pp.

Grinstein, Alexander. *The Index of Psychoanalytic Writings.* New York: International Universities Press, 1956–1969. 2802 pp.

Leland, Henry and Marilyn W. Deutsch. *Abnormal Behavior: A Guide to Information Sources.* Detroit, MI: Gale Research, 1980. 261 pp.

Menninger, Karl. *A Guide to Psychiatric Books in English.* 3d ed. New York: Grune & Stratton, 1972. 238 pp.

Morrow, William R. *Behavior Therapy Bibliography, 1950–1969: Annotated and Indexed.* Columbia: University of Missouri Press, 1971. 165 pp.

Strupp, Hans H. and Allan E. Bergin. *Research in Individual Psychotherapy: A Bibliography.* Chevy Chase, MD: U.S. National Institute of Mental Health, 1969. 169 pp.

F. Directories

American Psychiatric Association. *Biographical Directory of Fellows and Members.* New York: Bowker, 1941– .

III. Behavior

A. Encyclopedias, Handbooks

Ciminero, Anthony R., Karen S. Calhoun and Henry E. Adams, eds. *Handbook of Behavioral Assessment.* New York: Wiley-Interscience, 1977. 751 pp.

Ellis, Albert and Albert Abarbanel, eds. *The Encyclopedia of Sexual Behavior.* New 2d ed. New York: J. Aronson, 1973. 1072 pp.

Favell, Judith E. *The Power of Positive Reinforcement: A Handbook of Behavior Modification.* Springfield, IL: Thomas, 1977. 266 pp.

B. Review Serials, Yearbooks

Advances in Behavior Research and Therapy. v. 1– . Oxford, NY: Pergamon Press, 1977– .

Advances in the Study of Behavior. v. 1– . New York: Academic Press, 1965– .

Annual Review of Behavior Therapy: Theory and Practice. v. 1– . New York: Brunner/Mazel, 1973– .

Behavioral Group Therapy: An Annual Review. v. 1– . Champaign, IL: Research Press, 1979– .

Progress in Behavior Modification. v. 1– . New York: Academic Press, 1977– .

C. Periodical Indexes, Abstracting Services

Language and Language Behavior Abstracts. v. 1– . New York: Appleton-Century-Crofts, 1967– .

D. Bibliographies

Crabtree, Michael and Kenneth E. Moyer. *Bibliography of Aggressive Behavior: A Reader's Guide to the Research Literature.* New York: A.R. Liss, 1977–1981. 2 vols.

Davis, Martha. *Understanding Body Movement: An Annotated Bibliography.* New York: Arno, 1972. 190 pp.

Obadho, Constance E. *Human Nonverbal Behavior: An Annotated Bibliography.* Westport, CT: Greenwood, 1979. 196 pp.

IV. Child Development, Adolescence, Retardation

A. Encyclopedias, Handbooks

Adelson, Joseph, ed. *Handbook of Adolescent Psychology.* New York: Wiley, 1980. 624 pp.

Allen, Robert M. and Sue P. Allen. *Intellectual Evaluation of the Mentally Retarded Child: A Handbook.* Rev. ed. Los Angeles, CA: Western Psychological Services, 1975. 73 pp.

Brackbill, Yvonne, ed. *Infancy and Early Childhood: A Handbook and Guide to Human Development.* New York: Free Press, 1967. 523 pp.

Carmichael, Leonard. *Carmichael's Manual of Child Psychology.* 3d ed. New York: Wiley, 1970. 2 vols.

Ellis, Norman R., ed. *Handbook of Mental Deficiency: Psychological Theory and Research.* 2d ed. Hillsdale, NJ: Erlbaum, 1979. 785 pp.

Goslin, David A., ed. *Handbook of Socialization Theory and Research.* Chicago: Rand-McNally, 1968. 1182 pp.

Gruenberg, Sidonie M., ed. *The Encyclopedia of Child Care and Guidance.* Rev. ed. New York: Doubleday, 1963. 2 vols.

Johnson, Orval G. *Tests and Measurements in Child Development, Handbook II.* San Francisco: Jossey-Bass, 1976. 2 vols.

Noshspitz, Joseph D., ed. *Basic Handbook of Child Psychiatry.* New York: Basic Books, 1979. 4 vols.

Osofsky, Joy E. *Handbook of Infant Development.* New York: Wiley-Interscience, 1979. 954 pp.

Wolman, Benjamin B., James Egan and Alan O. Ross, eds. *Handbook of Treatment of Mental Disorders in Childhood and Adolescence.* Englewood Cliffs, NJ: Prentice-Hall, 1978. 475 pp.

Wolman, Benjamin B., ed. *Manual of Childhood Psychopathology.* New York: McGraw-Hill, 1972. 1380 pp.

Wright, Logan, Arlene B. Schaefer, and Gerald Solomons. *Encyclopedia of Pediatric Psychology.* Baltimore: University Park Press, 1979. 933 pp.

B. Review Serials, Yearbooks

Advances in Behavioral Pediatrics. v. 1– . Greenwich, CT: JAI Press, 1980– .

Advances in Child Development and Behavior. v. 1– . New York: Academic Press, 1963– .

Advances in Clinical Child Psychology. v. 1– . New York: Plenum, 1977– .

Advances in Developmental Psychology. v. 1– . Hillsdale, NJ: Erlbaum, 1981– .

Annual Progress in Child Psychiatry and Child Development. v. 1– . New York: Brunner/Mazel, 1968– .

International Review of Research in Mental Retardation. v. 1– . New York: Academic Press, 1966– .

C. Periodical Indexes, Abstracting Services

Child Development Abstracts and Bibliography. v. 1– . Chicago, IL: Society for Research in Child Development, 1927– .

Developmental Disabilities Abstracts. v. 1– . Bethesda, MD: National Institute of Mental Health, 1964– . (Formerly *Mental Retardation Abstracts.*)

D. Bibliographies

Benson, Hazel B. *Behavior Modification and the Child: An Annotated Bibliography.* Westport, CT: Greenwood Press, 1979. 398 pp.

Berlin, Irving N. *Bibliography of Child Psychiatry and Child Mental Health: With a Selected List of Films, An Official Publication of the Academy of Child Psychiatry.* 2d ed. New York: Human Sciences Press, 1976.

Brackbill, Yvonne, ed. *Research in Infant Behavior: A Cross-indexed Bibliography of Articles and Books Published 1950–1969.* Baltimore, MD: Williams & Wilkins, 1964. 281 pp.

Brown, Daniel G. *Behavior Modification in Child and School Mental Health: An Annotated Bibliography on Applications with Parents and Teachers and Family Counseling.* Champaign, IL: Research Press Co., 1972. 105 pp.

Myers, Hector F., Phyllis G. Rana, and Marcia Harris, comps. *Black Child Development in America, 1927–1977: An Annotated Bibliography.* Westport, CT: Greenwood Press, 1979. 470 pp.

Schulman, Janice B. and Robert C. Prall. *Normal Child Development: An Annotated Bibliography of Articles and Books Published 1950-1969.* New York: Grune and Stratton, 1971. 326 pp.

U.S. President's Panel on Mental Retardation. *Bibliography of World Literature on Mental Retardation, January 1940–March 1963.* Washington, DC: U.S. Dept. of Health, Education, and Welfare, Public Health Service, 1963. 564 pp. *Supplement, March 1963–December 31, 1964.* 1965. 99 pp.

V. Comparative Psychology, Animal Psychology

A. Handbooks

Handbook of Behavioral Neurobiology. v. 1– . New York: Plenum Press, 1978– .

B. Review Serials, Yearbooks

Advances in the Study of Behavior. v. 1– . New York: Academic Press, 1965– .

C. Periodical Indexes, Abstracting Services

Animal Behaviour Abstracts. v. 1– . London: Informational Retrieval Limited, 1974– .
Biological Abstracts. v. 1– . Philadelphia: BioSciences Information Service of Biological Abstracts, 1926– .
Science Citation Index. v. 1– . Philadelphia: Institute for Scientific Information, 1961– .

VI. Educational Psychology, Motivation, Learning

A. Encyclopedias, Handbooks

Arnold, Darlene B., and K.O. Doyle. *Education/ Psychology Journals: A Scholar's Guide.* Metuchen, NJ: Scarecrow Press, 1975. 143 pp.
Cofer, Charles N. *Human Motivation, A Guide to Information Sources.* Detroit: Gale Research Co., 1980. 176 pp.
Deighton, L.D., ed. *The Encyclopedia of Education.* New York: Macmillan, 1971. 10 vols.
Du Bois, Nelson F., George F. Alverson and Richard K. Staley. *Educational Psychology and Instructional Decisions.* Homewood, IL: Dorsey Press, 1979. 796 pp.
Handbook of Learning and Cognitive Processes. New Jersey: Erlbaum, 1975– .
Kennedy, James R. *Library Research Guide to Education.* Ann Arbor, MI: Pierian Press, 1979. 80 pp.
Mauser, August J. *Assessing the Learning Disabled: Selected Instruments.* 2d ed. San Rafael, CA: Academic Therapy Publications, 1977. 109 pp.

B. Dictionaries

Good, Carter V., ed. *Dictionary of Education.* 3d ed. New York: McGraw-Hill, 1973. 681 pp.

C. Review Serials, Yearbooks

Current Topics in Early Childhood Education. v. 1– . Norwood, NJ: Ablex, 1977– .
Glaser, Robert, ed. *Advances in Instructional Psychology.* Hillsdale, NJ: Erlbaum, 1978– .
Progress in Learning Disabilities. v. 1– . New York: Grune and Stratton, 1968– .
The Psychology of Learning and Motivation: Advances in Research and Theory. v. 1– . New York: Academic Press, 1967– .
Review of Educational Research. v. 1– . Washington: American Educational Research Association, 1931– .
Review of Research in Education. v. 1– . Itasca, IL: 1973– .
Yearbook of Special Education. 1980–81. 6th ed. Chicago: Marquis Academic Media, Marquis Who's Who, 1980. 442 pp.

D. Periodical Indexes, Abstracting Services

Child Development Abstracts and Bibliography. v. 1– . Chicago: University of Chicago Press, 1927– .
Current Index to Journals in Education. v. 1– . New York: CCM Information Services, 1969– .
Education Index. v. 1– . New York: H.W. Wilson, 1929– .
Exceptional Child Education Resources. v. 1– . New York: Council for Exceptional Children, 1969– .
Resources in Education. v. 1– . Washington, DC: Education Resources Information Center, 1966– .

E. Bibliographies

Berry, Dorothea M. *A Bibliographic Guide to Educational Research.* 2d ed. Metuchen, NJ: Scarecrow, 1980. 215 pp.
Hein, Ronald D., and Milo E. Bishop. *An Annotated Bibliography on Mainstreaming the Hearing Impaired, the Mentally Retarded and the Visually Impaired in the Regular Classroom.* Rochester, NY: National Technical Institute for the Deaf, 1978. 2 vols.

VII. Experimental Psychology, Research Techniques, Statistics

A. Handbooks

Bernstein, Allen L. *A Handbook of Statistics Solutions for the Behavioral Sciences.* New York: Holt, Reinhart & Winston, 1964. 145 pp.
Cattell, Raymond B., ed. *Handbook of Multivariate Experimental Psychology.* Chicago: Rand McNally, 1966. 959 pp.
Jung, John and Joan H. Bailey. *Contemporary Psychology Experiments: Adaptations for Laboratory.* 2d ed. New York: Wiley, 1976. 212 pp.
Miller, Delbert. *Handbook of Research Design and Social Measurement.* 3d ed. New York: McKay, 1977. 518 pp.
Walsh, John E. *Handbook of Nonparametric Statistics.* New York: Van Nostrand Reinhold, 1962. 3 vols.
Whitla, Dean K., ed. *Handbook of Measurement and Assessment in Behavioral Sciences.*

Reading, MA: Addison-Wesley, 1968. 508 pp.

B. Dictionaries

Kendall, Maurice G. and W.R. Buckland. *A Dictionary of Statistical Terms.* 3d ed., rev. and enl. London: Longman, 1975. 166 pp.

VIII. Guidance, Counselling, Communication, Psychology and Religion

A. Handbooks

Capps, Donald, Lewis Rambo and Paul Ransohoff. *Psychology of Religion: A Guide to Reference Sources.* Detroit: Gale Research Co., 1976. 352 pp.

Fretz, Bruce R. and David M. Mills. *Licensing and Certification of Psychologists and Counselors: A Guide to Current Policies, Procedures, and Legislation.* San Francisco: Jossey-Bass, 1980. 194 pp.

Gitter, A. George and Robert Grunin. *Communication: A Guide to Information Resources.* Detroit: Gale Research Co., 1980. 157 pp.

Lester, David, Betty H. Sell and Kenneth D. Sell. *Suicide: A Guide to Information Sources.* Detroit: Gale, 1980. 294 pp.

B. Review Serials, Yearbooks

Communication Yearbook. v. 1– . New Brunswick, NJ: Transaction Books, 1977– .

Review of Religious Research. v. 1– . New York: Religious Research Association, 1959– .

C. Periodical Indexes, Abstracting Services

Abstracts of Research in Pastoral Care and Counseling. v. 1– . National Clearinghouse, Joint Council on Research in Pastoral Care and Counseling, 1979– .

Pastoral Care and Counseling Abstracts. National Clearinghouse, Joint Council on Research in Pastoral Care and Counseling, 1972–1978. 7 vols.

Religion Index One: Periodicals. v. 1– . Chicago: American Theological Library Association, 1949– .

D. Bibliographies

Beit-Hallahmi, Benjamin. *Psychoanalysis and Religion: A Bibliography.* Norwood, PA: Norwood Editions, 1978. 182 pp.

Faberow, Norman L. *Bibliography on Suicide and Suicide Prevention, 1897-1957, 1958-1970.* Rockville, MD: National Institute of Mental Health, 1972. 107 pp.

Freeman, Ruth and Harrop A. Freeman. *Counseling: A Bibliography.* New York: Scarecrow, 1964. 986 pp.

Meissner, William W. *Annotated Bibliography in Religion and Psychology.* New York: Academy of Religion and Mental Health, 1961.

Stokes, G. Allison. "Bibliographies of Psychology/Religion Studies." *Religious Studies Review* 4 (1978), p. 273–279.

IX. History and Systems of Psychology

Murchison, Carl A., Edwin G. Boring and Gardner Lindzey, eds. *A History of Psychology in Autobiography.* v. 1– . New York: Appleton-Century-Crofts, 1930– .

Viney, Wayne, Michael Wertheimer and Marilyn Lou Wertheimer. *History of Psychology: A Guide to Information Sources.* Detroit: Gale Research, 1979. 502 pp.

Watson, Robert I. *Eminent Contributors to Psychology.* New York: Springer, 1974--76. 2 vols.

Watson, Robert I. *The History of Psychology and the Behavioral Sciences: A Bibliographic Guide.* New York: Springer, 1978. 241 pp.

Whitrow, Magda, ed. *ISIS Cumulative Bibliography: A Bibliography of the History of Science Formed from ISIS Critical Bibliographies 1–90, 1913--65.* v. 1– . London: Mansell, 1971--3. 1976. Supplement, 1965-1975. 1980.

Zusne, Leonard. *Names in the History of Psychology: A Biographical Sourcebook.* New York: Hemisphere, 1975. 489 pp.

X. Parapsychology

A. Encyclopedias, Handbooks

Cavendish, Richard, ed. *Encyclopedia of the Unexplained: Magic, Occultism and Parapsychology.* New York: McGraw-Hill, 1974. 304 pp.

Shepard, Leslie, ed. *Encyclopedia of Occultism and Parapsychology.* Detroit: Gale, 1978. 2 vols.

Walker, Benjamin. *Man and the Beast Within: The Encyclopedia of the Occult, the Esoteric, and the Supernatural.* New York: Stein and Day, 1977. 343 pp.

Wolman, Benjamin B., ed. *Handbook of Parapsychology.* New York: Van Nostrand Reinhold, 1977. 967 pp.

B. Bibliographies

White, Rhea A. and Laura A. Dale. *Parapsychology: Sources of Information.* Metuchen, NJ: Scarecrow, 1973. 302 pp.

White, Rhea A., comp. *Surveys in Parapsychology: Reviews of the Literature with Updated*

Bibliographies. Metuchen, NJ: Scarecrow, 1976. 484 pp.

XI. Personality

A. Handbooks

Borgatta, Edgar F. and William W. Lambert, eds. *Handbook of Personality Theory and Research.* Chicago: Rand McNally, 1968. 1232 pp.

Buros, Oscar K., ed. *Personality Tests and Reviews: Including an Index to the Mental Measurements Yearbooks.* Highland Park, NJ: Gryphon Press, 1970. 2 vols.

Cattell, Raymond and Ralph Dreger, eds. *Handbook of Modern Personality Theory.* Washington: Hemisphere, 1977. 804 pp.

B. Dictionaries

Heidenreich, Charles A. *A Dictionary of Personality: Behavior and Adjustment Terms.* Dubuque, IA: W.C. Brown, 1968. 213 pp.

C. Review Serials, Yearbooks

Progress in Experimental Personality Research. v. 1– . New York: Academic Press, 1964– .

XII. Physiological Psychology, Senses and Sensation, Drugs

A. Handbooks

Blackman, D.E. and D.J. Sanger, eds. *Contemporary Research in Behavioral Pharmacology.* New York: Plenum Press, 1978, 506 pp.

Butler, Francine. *Biofeedback: A Survey of the Literature.* New York: IFI/Plenum, 1978. 340 pp.

Dupont, Robert L., Avram Goldstein, and John O'Donnell, eds. *Handbook on Drug Abuse.* Washington, DC: National Institute on Drug Abuse, 1979. 452 pp.

Ford, D.H., J. Illari, and J.P. Schadé. *Atlas of the Human Brain.* 3d rev. and enl. ed. Amsterdam, NY: Elsevier North-Holland Biomedical Press, 1978. 299 pp.

Handbook of Physiology. Rev. ed. Bethesda, MD: American Physiological Society; Baltimore: Distributed by Williams and Wilkins. 1977– .

Iversen, Leslie L., Susan D. Iversen and Solomon H. Snyder, eds. *Handbook of Psychopharmacology.* New York: Plenum Press, 1975–1978. 14 vols.

Krauss, Stephen, ed. *Encyclopedic Handbook of Medical Psychology.* Boston: Butterworths, 1976. 585 pp.

Lingeman, Richard. *Drugs from A to Z: A Dictionary.* 2d rev. ed. New York: McGraw-Hill, 1974. 310 pp.

Miller, Richard A., and Ethel Burack. *Atlas of the Central Nervous System in Man.* 3d ed. Baltimore, MD: Williams and Wilkins, 1982. 81 pp.

Roberts, Melville and Joseph Hanaway. *Atlas of the Human Brain in Section.* Philadelphia: Lea and Febiger, 1970. 95 pp.

B. Review Serials, Yearbooks

Advances in Behavioral Pharmacology. v. 1– . New York: Academic Press, 1977– .

Advances in Psychobiology. v. 1– . New York: Wiley-Interscience, 1972– .

Annual Review of Neuroscience. v. 1– . Palo Alto, CA: Annual Reviews, 1978– .

Annual Review of Physiology. v. 1– . Stanford, CA: Annual Reviews, 1939– .

Biofeedback and Self-Control. v. 1– . Chicago: Aldine, 1977– .

Brill, Leon and Charles Winick, eds. *Yearbook of Substance Use and Abuse, Vol. II.* New York: Human Sciences Press, 1980. 360 pp.

Progress in Neurology and Psychiatry: An Annual Review. v. 1– . New York: Grune and Stratton, 1946– .

Progress in Psychobiology and Physiological Psychology. v. 1– . New York: Academic Press, 1976– . Continues *Progress in Physiological Psychology.* New York: Academic Press, 1966–1973.

Research Advances in Alcohol and Drug Problems. v. 1– . New York: Wiley Medical, 1974– .

C. Periodical Indexes, Abstracting Services

Index Medicus. v. 1– . Washington, DC: National Library of Medicine, 1950– .

Psychopharmacology Abstracts. v. 1– . Chevy Chase, MD: U.S. Dept. of Health, Education, and Welfare, National Institute of Mental Health, 1961– .

Science Citation Index. v. 1– . Philadelphia: Institute for Scientific Information, 1961– .

D. Bibliographies

Chalfant, H. Paul and Brent S. Roper, comps. *Social and Behavioral Aspects of Female Alcoholism: An Annotated Bibliography.* Westport, CT: Greenwood, 1980. 145 pp.

Emmett, Kathleen, and Peter Machamer. *Perception: An Annotated Bibliography.* New York: Garland, 1977. 177 pp.

XIII. Psychology of Aging

   A. Handbooks

   Birren, James E. and R. Bruce Sloane, eds. *Handbook of Mental Health and Aging*. Englewood Cliffs, NJ: Prentice-Hall, 1980. 1064 pp.
   Sourcebook on Aging. 2d ed. Chicago: Marquis Who's Who, 1979. 539 pp.

   B. Bibliographies

   Edwards, Willie M., and Frances Flynn, comps. *Gerontology: A Core List of Significant Works*. Ann Arbor, MI: Institute of Gerontology, University of Michigan-Wayne State University, 1978. 158 pp.
   McIlvaine, B., and Mohini Mundkur. *Aging: A Guide to Reference Sources, Journals and Government Publications*. Storrs: University of Connecticut Library, 1978. 162 pp.

XIV. Psychology of Women

   A. Encyclopedias

   Warren, Mary Ann. *The Nature of Women: An Encyclopedia and Guide to the Literature*. Inverness, CA: Edgepress, 1980. 708 pp.

   B. Abstracting Services

   Women Studies Abstracts. v. 1– . New York: Rush, 1972– .

   C. Bibliographies

   Ballou, Patricia K. *Women: A Bibliography of Bibliographies*. Boston: G.K. Hall, 1980. 155 pp.
   Zukerman, Elyse. *Changing Directions in the Treatment of Women: A Mental Health Bibliography*. Rockville, MD: National Institute of Mental Health, 1979. 494 pp.

XV. Social, Industrial, Organizational Psychology

   A. Handbooks

   Dunnette, Marvin E., ed. *Handbook of Industrial and Organizational Psychology*. Chicago: Rand McNally, 1976. 1740 pp.
   Encyclopedia of Sociology. Guildford, CT: Dushkin, 1974. 330 pp.
   Gottsegen, Gloria B. *Group Behavior: A Guide to Information Sources*. Detroit: Gale Research Co., 1979. 219 pp.
   Lindzey, Gardner and Elliot Aronson, eds. *The Handbook of Social Psychology*. 2d ed. v. 1–5. Reading, MA: Addison-Wesley, 1968–1969.
   March, James G., ed. *Handbook of Organizations*. Chicago: Rand McNally, 1965. 1247 pp.
   McMillan, Patricia and James R. Kennedy, Jr. *Library Research Guide to Sociology*. Ann Arbor, MI: Pierian Press, 1981. 70 pp.
   Slawski, Carl J. *Social Psychological Theories: A Comparative Handbook for Students*. Glenview, IL: Scott, Foresman, 1981. 188 pp.

   B. Dictionaries

   Hopke, William E. *Dictionary of Personnel and Guidance Terms; Including Professional Agencies and Associations*. Chicago: J.G. Ferguson, 1968. 464 pp.

   C. Review Serials, Yearbooks

   Advances in Experimental Social Psychology. v. 1– . New York: Academic Press, 1964– .
   Annual Review of Sociology. v. 1– . Palo Alto, CA: Annual Reviews, 1975– .
   Bickman, Leonard, ed. *Applied Social Psychology Annual*. v. 1– . Beverly Hills, CA: Sage, 1980– .
   Fishbein, Martin, ed. *Progress in Social Psychology*. v. 1– . Hillsdale, NJ: Erlbaum, 1980– .
   Rehabilitation Literature. v. 1– . Chicago: National Easter Seal Society for Crippled Children and Adults, 1940– . (1940–1955 entitled Bulletin on *Current Literature: Interest to Workers for the Handicapped*.)
   Research Annual on Intergroup Relations. v.1– . Chicago: Quadrangle Books, 1966– .
   Research in Organizational Behavior: An Annual Series of Analytical Essays and Critical Reviews. v. 1– . Greenwich, CT: JAI Press, 1979– .

   D. Periodical Indexes, Abstracting Services

   Personnel Management Abstracts. v. 1– . Ann Arbor, MI: Graduate School of Business Administration, University of Michigan, 1955– .
   Sociological Abstracts. v. 1– . New York: Sociological Abstracts, 1953– .
   Wile, Annadel N., ed. *C.R.I.S.: The Combined Retrospective Index Set to Journals in Sociology, 1895–1974*. 6 vols. Washington: Carrollton Press, 1978.

   E. Bibliographies

   De Grazia, Alfred, ed. *Public Opinion, Mass Behavior, and Political Psychology; An Anno-

tated and Intensely Indexed Compilation of Significant Books, Pamphlets and Articles. Princeton, NJ: Princeton Research, 1969. 1225 pp.

Morrison, Denton E., and Kenneth E. Hornback. *Collective Behavior: A Bibliography.* New York: Garland, 1976. 534 pp.

Walsh, Ruth and Stanley Birkin, eds. *Job Satisfaction and Motivation: An Annotated Bibliography.* Westport, CT: Greenwood Press, 1979. 643 pp.

XVI. Tests and Measurements

A. Handbooks

Andrulis, Richard S. *Adult Assessment: A Source Book of Tests and Measures of Human Behavior.* Springfield, IL: Thomas, 1977. 325 pp.

Beere, Carole E. *Women and Women's Issues: A Handbook of Tests and Measures.* San Francisco: Jossey-Bass, 1979. 550 pp.

Buros, Oscar K., ed. *The Eighth Mental Measurements Yearbook.* Highland Park, NJ: Gryphon Press, 1978. 2 vols.

Buros, Oscar K., ed. *Intelligence Tests and Reviews: A Monograph Consisting of the Intelligence Sections of the Seven Mental Measurements Yearbooks (1938-72) and Tests in Print II (1974).* Highland Park, NJ: Gryphon Press, 1975. 1129 pp.

Buros, Oscar K., ed. *Tests in Print II; An Index to Tests, Test Reviews and the Literature on Specific Tests.* Highland Park, NJ: Gryphon Press, 1974. 1107 pp.

Chun, Ki-Taek, Sidney Cobb, and John R. P. French. *Measures for Psychological Assessment: A Guide to 3,000 Original Sources and Their Applications.* Ann Arbor: Survey Research Center, Institute for Social Research, University of Michigan, 1975. 664 pp.

Goldman, Bert A. and John L. Saunders. *Directory of Unpublished Experimental Mental Measures.* v. 1– . New York: Behavioral Publications, 1974– .

Lake, Dale G., Matthew B. Miles and Ralph B. Earle. *Measuring Human Behavior: Tools for the Assessment of Social Functioning.* New York: Teachers College Press, 1973. 422 pp.

Standards for Educational and Psychological Tests. Washington, DC: American Psychological Association, 1974. 40 pp.

Straus, Murray A. and Bruce W. Brown. *Family Measurement Techniques: Abstracts of Published Instruments, 1935-1974.* Rev. ed. Minneapolis: University of Minnesota Press, 1978. 668 pp.

B. Dictionaries

A Glossary of Measurement Terms: A Basic Vocabulary for Evaluation and Testing. Rev. ed. Monterey, CA: CTB/McGraw-Hill, 1973. 23 pp.

D. Review Serials

McReynolds, Paul, ed. *Advances in Psychological Assessment.* v. 1– . Palo Alto, CA: Science and Behavior Books, 1968– .

APPENDIX V

GUIDELINES FOR PROCEEDING

This brief summary is designed to help you check your progress as you work on a research paper. It will be most useful to you if you have completely read this book and now just need a few quick reminders on the process before starting your latest research paper.

1. Choose a topic that interests you. (Chapter 1)

    Use specialized encyclopedias from Chapter 1 or Appendix IV to find an overview of your topic and narrow the focus of your paper. Encyclopedias also usually include short bibliographies you can pursue in the card catalog.

2. Check the card catalog for books. (Chapter 2)

    Use *Library of Congress Subject Headings* first, taking advantage of the "see" and "see also" references to zero in on the most useful headings; also look up the books from the encyclopedia bibliographies and you may be able to use subject headings printed on their cards. Try to use the information on the catalog card to help you determine which books to look for on the shelves.

3. Use review serials for an overview of more current research. (Chapter 3)

    Choose an appropriate review serial with the help of Chapter 3, Appendix IV, or your reference librarian.

4. Start reading the published research reports on your topic, finding the reports through an indexing or abstracting service especially *Social Sciences Index* and *Psychological Abstracts*. (Chapter 4)

    Use Chapter 4 to determine which index or abstract service is most likely to cover your topic, but remember that you'll get the best results by checking more than one. In Appendix IV there are lists of more specialized indexes and abstracts, and your reference librarian can help you find others. If your time is short or your topic is complex, you may want to try a computerized literature search.

5. After you've studied some research reports, you may want to pursue prominent researchers through name indexes. (Chapter 5)

    Social Sciences Citation Index has the most comprehensive approach to names. It also contains information on who cited an author's work, which will lead you to still more research.

6. To find the very latest published research, use *Current Contents*. (Chapter 6)

    Current Contents not only prints the contents pages of periodicals, but also gives an author and subject approach before the periodicals reach the regular indexing services.

7. You may need to use other, more selective guides to the literature in specific areas of psychology. Chapter 7 explains a few guides, and more are listed in Appendix IV or can be recommended by your reference librarian.

8. For medical and psychiatric topics, *Index Medicus* is valuable (Appendix II)

9. United States government documents contain an amazing amount of valuable research in psychology. They may be located in a special part of your library and may not show up in the card catalog. Appendix III explains how to use government documents, and your reference librarian can help you find them in your library.

10. If your library does not have all the materials you need, there are alternatives. (Chapter 8)

    Often you can visit other libraries to use materials, though you usually cannot check them out. In some cases, the library can borrow materials for you through interlibrary loan, or you can have some pages photocopied. Chapter 8 and your reference librarian can help you with details.

11. For help in the style and format of actually writing your paper, look at the "Handbooks for writing psychology papers" section in Appendix IV, or ask your professor or reference librarian.

Index of Titles

Note: This index includes only the *reference* sources treated in the twelve chapters. It excludes non-reference books and works cited only in the appendices.

Annual Review of Psychology 13-15
Current Contents 33-36
Guide to Library Research in Psychology 37-38
Guide to Reference Books. Supplement. 37, 40
Guide to Reference Material. 37
Index Medicus. 24, 27, 45-47
International Encyclopedia of Psychiatry, Psychology, Psychoanalysis & Neurology. 2-5, 31
International Encyclopedia of the Social Sciences. 4-5
Library of Congress Subject Headings. 8-11
Monthly Catalog of United States Government Publications. 48-49
Psychological Abstracts. 17-27, 29
Readers' Guide to Periodical Literature. 17-18, 43
Social Sciences Citation Index. 23-27
Social Sciences Citation Index "Permuterm Index." 17, 23, 27
Social Sciences Citation Index "Source Index." 23
Social Sciences Index. 17-18, 23, 27, 29
Sociological Abstracts. 17, 22, 23, 26-27, 29
Sources of Information in the Social Sciences: A Guide to the Literature. 37, 39
Subject Catalog. 41-42
Thesaurus of Psychological Index Terms. 19-21, 23, 25, 27

Notes

Notes

Notes